EXECUTED
AT DAWN

EXECUTED
AT DAWN

BRITISH FIRING
SQUADS ON THE
WESTERN FRONT
1914–1918

DAVID JOHNSON

In memory of my mother
Winifred Johnson
11 January 1923–21 February 2014

First published 2015

by Spellmount, an imprint of The History Press
The Mill, Brimscombe Port
Stroud, Gloucestershire, GL5 2QG
www.thehistorypress.co.uk

British Library Cataloguing in Publication Data.
A catalogue record for this book is available from the British Library.

ISBN 978 0 7509 5917 9

Typeset in Bembo 11/13pt by The History Press
Printed and bound in Great Britain by TJ International Ltd

CONTENTS

Introduction   9

1   The Organisation of the Executions:
    The Regulatory Framework   15
2   The Selection of the Firing Squad   46
3   The Firing Squad   59
4   The Army Chaplain   81
5   The Medical Officer   94
6   The Military Police and the Assistant Provost Marshal   98
7   Abolition of the Death Penalty in the British Army   107
8   The Campaign for Pardons for Those Executed   129

Conclusion   154

Appendix 1: Statement Made by Dr John Reid,
    Armed Forces Minister, on 24 July 1998   173
Appendix 2: Written Ministerial Statement by
    Des Browne, Secretary of State for Defence,
    on 18 September 2006   179
Appendix 3: Report of an Adjournment Debate
    Held in the House of Commons on 3 March 2009:
    The Story of Private James Smith   182
Appendix 4: The Last Letter Home from Private Albert
    Troughton of the 1st Royal Welch Fusiliers, who was
    Executed on 22 April 1915, Having Been Found
    Guilty of Desertion   198

Bibliography   200
Index   204

For Those Shot For Cowardice

by A.R. (David) Lewis

Their voices echo down the years, demanding justice:
'It's the noise, echoing, rebounding in the muddy trenches,
the shells continuous, shrieking, exploding in front and rear.'
I just wandered off, not knowing who, or what I was.
I'm not afraid to die, it's living in this hell,
that causes the problem – I start to shake – my mind
   goes dead.'
Then the finger pointing General 'No time for cowards,
court martial them. Stamp out this cancer'
Court martial's obligatory verdict guilty – punishment death.
Shell shock – trauma – just excuses for cowards.
Then the voices of the firing squads are also heard.
'The poor devil was legless, his brain already dead.
His bowels running out of control. He called for his Mam,
as we tied him to the chair he talked to her'
'What are they doing to me, Mam?
I can't see you, Mam, they have covered my eyes.
Sorry Mam, I have messed myself. Help me, Mam.'
The executioners once more, 'What a way to die,
his blood mingling with the filth in his trousers.
God forgive me my part in his death.'
And still the voices of the dead cry out.
'I'm not a coward – no blindfold for me,
I will look death full in the face – I am not guilty.
Shot as a coward, no pension for my wife.'

Dead – Not Dishonoured

by A.R. (David) Lewis

At four in the morning, the shelling restarted.
Their shrieking and screaming, the only sound heard.
Stand to at five, advance at five thirty.
Knee deep in mud the soldiers waited,
to hear the whistle, the command to advance.
The young lad waited, head bowed, trembling.
Praying 'Please let's go – get out of this noise.'
Lips not moving, mind chanting 'Let's go, let's go.'
Not afraid to charge forward to meet his fate,
the mud, the noise, the waiting caused his trauma.
The enemy now returned the shelling, increasing the bedlam,
adding the crunch and exploding noises.
The Soldiers cursed, and finished their smokes.
The young one now visibly shaking, not in control.
He dropped his rifle, turned and ran.
The regulation court martial just a formality.
The verdict 'Guilty'. The sentence 'Death.'
Shell shock not mentioned, cowardice was.
The dishonoured young man to die at dawn.
His breakfast half a mug of rum, and five bullets to follow.

David Lewis is a prolific writer of prose and poetry (visit www.proprose.co.uk) who was born in 1919 and served with the Welsh Guards from 1938 to 1946, taking in both Dunkirk and the Normandy landings. David Lewis has kindly contributed three of his poems, which I am proud to include in this book. With his agreement, I have included two of these on the preceding pages and the third can be found at the end of the book. David has maintained a long-standing interest in the Shot at Dawn campaign, which he still considers to have some unfinished business in the sense that the complete story has not yet been told.

INTRODUCTION

In 2009 I went on a tour of the Western Front, visiting Ypres, Passchendaele, the Messines Ridge, Ploegsteert, Arras, Vimy Ridge and the Somme, and I saw the execution post at Poperinghe. Reading about those places is one thing, but actually to be there is a truly powerful experience that I would recommend to anyone. Words cannot describe the emotional effect of visiting the immaculately maintained

Poperinghe New Military Cemetery. As a major military centre just behind the lines that was relatively safe and close to Ypres, the town of Poperinghe (now Poperinge) was the location of numerous courts martial and executions. (Courtesy of Paul Kendall, author of *Aisne 1914* and *Bullecourt 1917*)

military cemeteries with their rows and rows of white head-stones stretching off into the distance, or indeed attending the moving ceremony held at the Menin Gate in Ypres every evening. The headstones mark the final resting place of thousands of men killed in action, but in addition they also contain the graves of those who were executed, shot at dawn, by the British Army.

† † †

In the First World War, 302 British and Commonwealth soldiers, representing about one in ten of those condemned, were executed for military offences committed whilst on active service on the Western Front (Babington, 2002) and we know the names and the circumstances of those shot thanks to the research of Julian Putkowski and Julian Sykes in *Shot at Dawn*, first published in 1989, and that of Cathryn Corns and John Hughes-Wilson in *Blindfold and Alone* in 2001.

The books written so far have tended to focus on the controversy surrounding their cases and the court martial processes involved, and therefore it is not my intention in this book to go over that ground again, except where it is necessary for contextual purposes. My focus is on military executions post-confirmation of the sentence, and it seems appropriate therefore that the book should consider the issues of abolition and pardons. In doing this the book will examine the executions from the perspective of the members of the firing squad, the officers in charge, the army chaplains, the medical officers and the others who would have been present apart from those who took part, because, unsurprisingly, much less is known about them.

Soldiers have always had a natural reticence to speak to their families about the fighting that they have been involved in and the horrors that they have witnessed. If speaking about killing the enemy is so difficult, then how much harder it would have been to speak about witnessing or taking part in the execution of one of your own, perhaps even someone that you had known or had enlisted with in one of the so-called 'pals battalions'. It is almost impossible to imagine what it must have been like living with those images in your mind – particularly in smaller communities where relatives and friends of the deceased may have frequented the same shops, factories and public houses as you, and as a result may have asked you awkward questions in an effort to find out how a loved one had died.

Unfortunately many of those who took part in British military executions were themselves killed in later combat and therefore the story of their involvement may be thought to have died with them. However, it has been possible to discover some of their names and some of their stories. Investigating events that took place a century ago means that there are now no opportunities for primary research, as even those who fought and survived are now all dead, and the opportunity to speak to them has long passed. This book, therefore, relies on secondary research drawing on what has already been published, together with personal and regimental diaries and letters, where these exist. It is through that research that the book will seek to explore and tell the stories of how those involved were selected, how they were treated before, during, and after the executions, and why there appears to have been so many procedural variations in the way that the executions were conducted on the Western Front.

I believe that all research must have a question at its heart, and it is this last point that fulfils that role. The British Army was at the time of the First World War, as it is now, a highly regulated organisation, with the smallest detail of army life set out in the Army Acts, military law and the King's Regulations, and so it is not unreasonable to assume that executions would have been regulated and consistent, in accordance with a form of established 'standard operating procedure', to ensure that they were conducted as humanely as possible.

In turn, it would not be unreasonable to ask why a century later this might still be of interest to anyone. The truthful response is that although this book will not change anything,

I believe it is a worthwhile subject to explore because it will add to the knowledge and understanding of yet another aspect of the First World War. Executions are an aspect of the First World War that still remains a source of discomfort to many, and yet they are a part of the story of that conflict and continue to cast their long shadow over a century later.

The book will also discuss the related issues of the abolition of the death penalty in the British Army and the campaign to secure pardons for those executed.

In addition, there is a link between this book and my previous one (*One Soldier and Hitler, 1918*, hardback/ *The Man Who Didn't Shoot Hitler*, paperback), which is a biography of Private Henry Tandey, VC, DCM, MM, the most decorated British private soldier to survive the First World War. In that book I wrote about the case of Drummer Frederick Rose of the 2nd Battalion of the Yorkshire Regiment (later to be known as the Green Howards) who was executed for desertion.

Drummer Rose would almost certainly have been known to Henry, as they served in the same battalion and would have headed off to Flanders together in August 1914. However, in December 1914 Rose had deserted his battalion and remained absent until December 1916. He was sentenced to death and executed by firing squad on 4 March 1917, by which time Henry was hospitalised in Britain for treatment to a wound received at the Battle of the Somme. Therefore, he was spared having to witness, or even be a member of, the firing squad. But it made me realise how close Henry had come to being part of one of these executions. As Henry did not appear to have kept a diary, sent letters to family or friends, or talked to them about his experiences, it is impossible to know his views on the death penalty or of taking part in a firing squad, but it set me thinking, and the result is this book.

I have not set out to be judgemental about the individuals that have been identified because they were largely behaving according to the standards of the time. I approached this book from a neutral position, allowing the theory or narrative to emerge from the research, and what I started to find was that there is still much to be debated about the conduct and behaviour of the British Army and politicians, not just in the war years but in the subsequent decades too.

† † †

Whilst writing, a number of times I have experienced the feeling of reaching a plateau in my work. I have been in this position enough times to know that something is needed to push my work onto the next level, and fortunately something always seems to come along that provides that necessary impetus. In this case it happened at a time when my work, while not exactly stalled, could be said to be progressing slowly, and my thoughts by way of self-distraction turned to whom I could ask to write the foreword. Eventually, through researching the Shot at Dawn campaign, I made contact with Mac Macdonald of the organisation FLOW (Forces Literary Organisation Worldwide), which has as its mission:

> To help anyone who has suffered from the effects of war, including the suffering shared by family members and friends too.

The organisation believes, based on research that proves its therapeutic value, that the writing of a poem or a piece of prose provides an opportunity to release deep emotions in a safe environment, and that reading what others have written helps individuals to take comfort from the thought that others have been through similar experiences. The website is well worth a visit: www.flowforall.org.

FLOW's website includes some material from the Shot at Dawn campaign and, with the help of Mac Macdonald, I was able to contact Mr A.R. (David) Lewis who was very supportive of my work on this subject and as a result gave me his generous permission to use his poems in this book. I am also very grateful to Mac Macdonald for passing on to me a file of documents relating to the Shot at Dawn campaign.

Many other people have generously helped me, and thanks and acknowledgements are due to the following:

John Hughes-Wilson, David Blake (Museum of Army Chaplaincy), Richard Callaghan (Royal Military Police Museum), Julian Putkowski, Scott Flaving (Yorkshire Regiment), Shaun Barrington, Jo de Vries and Rebecca Newton (The History Press), Mainstream Publishing for permission to quote from *To War with God* by Peter Fiennes, Colin Williams and Neil Cobbett at The National Archives, the staff at the National Army Museum, and last but not least my wife Val.

I have made all reasonable efforts to ensure that all quotations within this book have been included with the full consent of the copyright holders. In the event that copyright holders had not responded prior to publication, then should they so wish, they are invited to contact the publishers so that any necessary corrections may be made in any future editions of this book.

I believe that all research must inevitably raise more questions than it answers, and I hope that others may be motivated to debate and further research the issues raised in this book, and to come forward with any additional evidence that will either confirm or disprove my analysis.

David Johnson

1

THE ORGANISATION OF THE EXECUTIONS: THE REGULATORY FRAMEWORK

The condemned man had spent his last night on this earth in a small room that was barely furnished with a table, two chairs and a straw bed. By the light of a guttering candle he had written his final, painful letters to his family and friends, and laid out his few personal possessions on the table. The small room was further diminished in size by the presence of two guards, who stood with bayonets fixed by the door and the single window to prevent his escape.

Occasionally through the night, the chaplain came to spend time with him, but otherwise he sat alone with his thoughts. With his letters written, he decided that he would spend his last hours awake and, so, moving his chair so that he could watch for the approach of dawn through the window, he started on the bottle of rum that had been left on the table. Inevitably, he fell asleep, only to be roused by the sound of footsteps and voices outside the door.

It was just before dawn and the sky was starting to get light as a small group of men was marched into an unused quarry. They were then left to stand around smoking and looking anywhere but at each other, not wanting to catch another's eye, the smoke from their cigarettes and pipes drifting upwards to add to the slight mistiness of the morning. Some stared at the ground, some examined their hands, and some stared into the middle distance. Most definitely, nobody wanted to speak, as they all knew what they were there to do.

A short distance away stood the lonely figure of the young lieutenant in charge of the firing party, his face pale from the knowledge of what was to come. He smoked ferociously and stamped his feet in an effort to keep warm while he nervously checked and re-checked his service revolver, worried that this morning of all mornings it might jam.

Two companies of the condemned man's regiment then marched silently into the quarry and took up position across its open end, and, in response to a shouted order, stood at ease.

Soon, too soon for some, they heard the approach of a vehicle, and a motor ambulance appeared at the edge of the quarry. The members of the firing squad were then called to attention, facing away from the stake that none of them had been able to look at, with their rifles placed on a tarpaulin on the ground behind them.

The condemned man, thankfully very drunk and therefore apparently senseless as to what was about to happen, was all but carried from the back of the ambulance by two military police-men, accompanied by an army chaplain. The man was so drunk that his arms did not need to be tied behind his back or his legs bound at his ankles as he made the short, stumbling walk to the stake supported by the military policemen. On arrival at the stake, and held between the two beefy redcaps, his arms were momentarily released before being tied behind it, but being drunk, he could not feel the rough surface against the skin of his wrists and hands. A further binding held his ankles to the stake. As the man drunkenly muttered to himself, a blindfold was placed over his eyes and the medical officer stepped forward to pin a small, white square of fabric over his heart.

Meanwhile, the lieutenant had loaded a single round of ammunition into each rifle with the help of an assistant prov-ost marshal, and then mixed them up. As was usually the case, one of the rounds was a blank. When the rifles were ready, the lieutenant took up his position and signalled to the chaplain to begin saying the condemned man's final prayer. The assistant provost marshal, by a pre-arranged and silent signal, ordered the firing squad to turn, pick up their rifles, and prepare to fire as each worked the bolts of their rifles with trembling hands. At the same time the watching companies of men were brought to attention. When the rifles were ready, the lieutenant took up his position and signalled to the chaplain to finish the condemned man's final prayer.

The chaplain solemnly intoned 'Amen' and turned and walked away with his head bowed. The lieutenant then unsheathed his sword and raised it in the air. Fingers tightened on triggers and when the sword was lowered a thunderous volley rang out. Some bullets, whether deliberately or as a result of incompetence, missed the staked figure completely and threw up spurts of dust from the quarry wall behind. Some found their target and the condemned man sagged forward, at which point the medical officer approached him to determine whether life had been extinguished. With a look of disgust he signalled to the lieutenant that the man was still alive. The lieutenant, with a trembling hand, then stepped forward to finish him off with a revolver shot through the side of the head.

The watching companies were swiftly marched out of the quarry, with their sergeants silently defying them from looking anywhere but straight ahead. The firing squad was then brought to attention and marched back to its breakfast, also without a sideways glance at the dead man, followed by the lieutenant, the assistant provost marshal, the military policemen and the medical officer. They left two ambulance bearers to take down the body, which was then wrapped in a cape ready for burial, and to clear away the bloodied straw from around the stake. When they were finished, they placed the body on a stretcher and carried it to the burial site, where the chaplain presided over a short funeral service.

What you have just read is my fictional account of a British Army execution on the Western Front. It contains all the elements that you would expect, but how were these executions really organised and regulated?

✝ ✝ ✝

It is unlikely that those who went off to the Western Front could ever have imagined the horrors they would have to face, whatever their rank or experience. The men of the British Expeditionary Force, and those who volunteered in August 1914, were naively convinced as they cheerfully marched off to war that it would be over by Christmas, while the generals, equally naively, thought that the cavalry would prevail – indeed, right up until the final days of the war, Sir Douglas Haig, the commander-in-chief, was still looking for ways to unleash his cavalry on the Germans. Nobody foresaw that this would be a more static war of trenches, mud, machine guns, barbed wire and artillery barrages.

Soldiers going to the Western Front and to the other theatres of the First World War would have been trained in the very many ways to kill the enemy using their rifles, bayonets, grenades, machine guns and artillery, yet nothing could really have prepared those men for the actual sights, sounds and conditions that they would encounter. Despite their training, throughout the war many British soldiers still could not bring themselves to shoot wounded, unarmed and retreating German soldiers, so how could that training help if they were unlucky enough to be involved as a member of a firing squad, brought together to execute one of their own? What would that have felt like? Thankfully, very few people will ever have such an experience and so we will have to use our imagination to try to understand and gain insight into that situation.

When the state decides to take the life of one of its own citizens, in what can be described as an act of judicial murder, it is a momentous judgement for all concerned. Who decided how that execution should be conducted and who should be present – or was it simply left to the individual whims and preferences of the assistant provost marshal or the commanding officers?

† † †

Those who volunteered for the army in August 1914, and those who joined afterwards, either as volunteers or as conscripts, left the civilian world behind them and found themselves in an alien environment, subject to what now seems, 100 years later, harsh military law which governed all aspects of the lives of the officers and soldiers in peace and in war, at home or overseas.

As a result of the outbreak of war, in September 1914 the normal system of military court martial was replaced by a system of summary court martial. Offences that carried the death penalty were then to be dealt with by a field general court martial presided over by a minimum of three officers, one of whom had to hold at least the rank of captain in order to act as president. All three had to be in agreement on any sentence passed. The recommended sentence was then passed up the chain of command, together with any mitigating circumstances and pleas for clemency.

The changes made in September 1914 are important because they allowed for the sentence, passed by the field general court martial, to be carried out within twenty-four hours – with no right of appeal. The reality for those sentenced to death was that the passage of time from sentence to its promulgation or announcement could be weeks if not months, whereas the time between promulgation and the actual execution was normally just a matter of a few hours.

On 8 September 1914, for example, Private Thomas Highgate at the age of 17 became the first British soldier to be executed on the Western Front for desertion, just two days after sentence had been passed, proving that the process could be quick. In fact, the time between Private Highgate being informed of the confirmation of his sentence and his execution was just forty-five minutes (David, 2013).

Driver Thomas Moore of the 24th Division Train (Army Service Corps, 4th Company) was executed on 26 February 1916, having been sentenced for murder, with his court martial having taken place on 18 February. The death sentence was only promulgated at 4.03 a.m., the company was paraded at 5.30 a.m., and just ten minutes later he was dead, which gave little time for any army chaplain to help him prepare for his end: Moore only had eighty-seven minutes from announcement to execution.

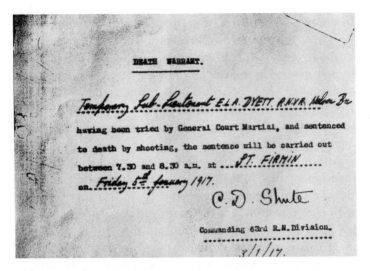

DEATH WARRANT.

Temporary Sub-Lieutenant E.L.A. DYETT. R.N.V.R. Nelson Bn

having been tried by General Court Martial, and sentenced
to death by shooting, the sentence will be carried out
between 7.30 and 8.30 a.m. at ...ST. FIRMIN....
on ...Friday 5th January 1917.

C.D. Shute

Commanding 63rd R.N. Division.

2/1/17.

Sub-Lieutenant Edwin Dyett (opposite) was informed that the sentence of death
had been passed upon him after he had returned to his battalion.

In contrast, the court martial for Sub-Lieutenant Edwin
Dyett of the Nelson Battalion, Royal Naval Division, was held
on 26 December 1916 for an alleged offence of desertion on
13 November (Moore, 1999). Under the Army Act, the fact
that at the end of those proceedings Sub-Lieutenant Dyett was
not released meant that he would have known that he had
been found guilty, but at that stage he would not have been
informed of the sentence, although he would have been aware
of the penalty for desertion. The procedure thereafter, which
had been set down in some detail, was, according to Moore:

- A character report from his company commander and an
  opinion as to whether the death sentence was appropriate
  in that case.
- A report from a medical officer as to his nervous condition.
- The commanders of the brigade, division, corps and army
  in which the individual's battalion was assigned had to
  submit their recommendation as to whether the death
  sentence was necessary.

In the meantime, Dyett was returned to his battalion, where he was given the role of censoring the men's letters. On 4 January 1917, while playing cards in the mess, he was told by an officer – in front of all those present – that a sentence of death had been confirmed by the commander-in-chief, Sir Douglas Haig. The execution took place on the 5th. It was to be a case that caused concern to many people, and was subsequently raised in Parliament.

Although Sub-Lieutenant Dyett's case did not merit a mention in the commander-in-chief's diaries (Sheffield and Bourne, 2005), there is an entry for 11 January 1917 that deals with eleven cases where the death penalty had been recommended. The eleven men were from the 35th Division and Haig confirmed the sentence on three of them: Lance-Sergeant William Stones and Lance-Corporals Peter Goggins and John McDonald, all from the 19th Durham Light Infantry. Where the rest were concerned, Haig commuted the sentence to fifteen years' penal servitude, which he then suspended.

† † †

The 302 British and Commonwealth soldiers executed for military offences committed while on active service on the Western Front (Babington, 2002), cast a long shadow and their cases remain controversial to this day. As shocking as that figure might be, it represents only 10 per cent of the 3,076 sentenced to death (in fact some 20,000 offences that could have attracted the death sentence were committed over this same period). These statistics show, therefore, that some of those executed were undoubtedly unlucky to be in the wrong place at the wrong time, when those further up the command chain saw a need to make an example of them, thereby making it something of a lottery for those concerned and therefore inherently unfair. This seems to have happened in the case of the eleven men mentioned above: although all of them had been found guilty, it was the three more senior men that Haig decided needed to face the ultimate penalty. It is a pity that the records of those whose sentences were commuted were destroyed in 1924 because it would be interesting to read the reasons given and to see where their cases differed from those who were executed.

A previous diary (Sheffield and Bourne) entry, for 3 March 1915, details briefly that Haig had confirmed the death sentence on three men 'of the Loyal North Lancs' who had deserted, stating the reason: 'The state of discipline in this battalion is not very satisfactory…' This entry, and the decision it describes, raise some interesting points. Firstly, it seems to be subjective because there is no detail as to the basis of Haig's conclusion about the state of the battalion's discipline. A battalion's discipline could encompass a broad spectrum of offences ranging from the soldiers' appearance up to a reluctance to fight, and Haig's diary entry does not clarify the shortcomings involved. Secondly, every soldier and officer in the battalion must therefore be considered to have borne a collective responsibility for the deaths of their three comrades because it is possible that, had the battalion displayed higher standards of discipline, they would have been spared, further highlighting the part that chance played in these matters.

As a final point about the number of sentences passed, it is also interesting to note that the British Army only executed thirty-seven men between 1865 and 1898 – during a time when it was fighting colonial wars all across the globe – and only four men during the whole of the Boer War from 1898 to 1902 (Irish Government Report, 2004). These statistics are important because they seem to imply that a significant increase in the prevalence of capital offences was caused by the horrors of the First World War. Although this undoubtedly played a part, it needs to be borne in mind that this was the first war for 100 years that saw the British Army fighting in Europe. This meant that, for many soldiers, home was just across the English Channel, making desertion an attractive option, whereas that would not normally have been the case if they were fighting in Africa or India. If you deserted then, where did you go?

† † †

In the early 1900s, court sentences were about punishment and deterrence, and society and the Church in general both accepted and supported capital punishment. In a civilian criminal court there could only be one sentence for the offence of murder, namely death, and once all the legal procedures were exhausted then the penalty was enacted. The situation in the military was different, and the vast majority of death sentences were passed for offences that would not be recognised as an offence in the civilian world.

With no right of appeal, the fate of the condemned man rested solely in the hands of his commander-in-chief, who would make his decision based on his view of the needs of the service rather than looking for mitigating reasons to commute the sentence. Those who did have their sentences commuted were either sent to prison or, in some cases, as a result of the Suspension of Sentences Act of 1915, the sentence would have been suspended and the individual returned to their unit with the certain knowledge that it could be enforced at any time. Where a sentence was suspended, the Act provided for the sentence to be reviewed at intervals of not more than three months, and if the individual's conduct merited it, then the sentence could be remitted, thereby introducing the possibility of rehabilitation.

The Army (Suspension of Sentences) Act of 1915 meant that those who had their sentences commuted would serve the alternative sentence when out of the front line. This Act: 'fulfilled the basic tenet of military law in that the penalty did nothing to precipitate a manpower shortage'.

An example of this can be found in a book by Lieutenant Max Plowman (2001) who had been a subaltern in the 10th Battalion, West Yorkshire Regiment. He had served on the Western Front, and wrote that a deserter from his regiment had his death sentence commuted to two years' hard labour, which he then served when out of the front line.

The First World War was fought in a dehumanising and brutal environment where individual life seemed increasingly to have little value except to the individual concerned and their family, friends and loved ones. Such an environment, then as now, also had the potential to lead to thoughtless actions and an emphasis on self-preservation. These, it could be argued, would also be present on the execution ground unless the procedure was regulated. So did the British Army, with its penchant for highly regulated ceremonial and an eye for detail, have in effect a 'standard operating procedure' to be followed for all executions, with nothing left to chance?

The Western Front from 1914 to 1918 was a world unlike any other that had gone before, or indeed came after, so there is always a potential risk of looking at it and judging it through today's eyes rather than by the standards of those times. The risk of subjectivity could be avoided by utilising a set of regulations setting out the conduct of an execution, if they existed, thereby providing an objective means of examining the roles and experiences of those who took part against the norms of that time.

† † †

The existence of the death penalty in the military can be traced back to the fourteenth century, and was based on the twin aims of maintaining discipline and not alienating the local population, but, as mentioned above, with the important proviso that it should not cause a shortage of men. These principles of discipline and not alienating the local population can be seen in the following document that was issued to every soldier for them to keep in their Active Service Pay Book (The National Archives, WO 95/1553/1):

> You are ordered abroad as a soldier of the King to help our French comrades against the invasion of a common enemy. You have to perform a task which will need your courage, your energy, your patience. Remember that the honour of the British Army depends on your individual conduct. It

will be your duty not only to set an example of discipline and perfect steadiness under fire but also to maintain the most friendly relations with those whom you are helping in this struggle. The operations in which you are engaged will, for the most part, take place in a friendly country, and you can do your own country no better service than in showing yourself in France and Belgium in the true character of a British soldier.

Be invariably courteous, considerate and kind. Never do anything likely to injure or destroy property, and always look upon looting as a disgraceful act. You are sure to be met with a welcome and be trusted; your conduct must justify that welcome and that trust. Your duty cannot be done unless your health is sound. So keep constantly on your guard against any excesses. In this new experience you may find temptations in wine and women. You must entirely resist both temptations, and, while treating all women with perfect courtesy, you should avoid any intimacy.

Do your duty bravely.

Fear God.

Honour the King

Kitchener

Field Marshal

This paper was then supplemented by a further exhortation from the brigade to which the men were attached, in this case the 13th Brigade (WO 95/1553/1):

We shall shortly, probably, be engaged with the enemy.

Remember that the Germans hate the bayonet, and also that their theory that 'determined men in sufficient numbers can do anything' has already been proved, at Liege, to be a fallacy. In the face of modern weapons they cannot.

Remember also that heavy artillery fire looks terrible, but is far more alarming than harmful, and if you do not bunch, it will not do much damage. The Germans do bunch, hence their enormous losses.

Therefore remember three things:

1. If stationary, keep cool and shoot straight and steadily.
2. If moving, keep good intervals and distances.
3. If the opportunity offers, use the bayonet with all the vigour you can.

And, above all, remember that no man in the 13th Brigade surrenders. We must fight to the end, for the honour of our Country, and the credit of our Brigade and our Regiments.

If these words came from the mouth of General Melchett in *Blackadder Goes Forth*, they would, at the very least, raise a smile from an audience today because of this document's seemingly comedic content. However, its author was deadly serious with the exhortation that 'no man in the 13th Brigade surrenders'. It is likely that it was this exhortation that sealed the fate of Private Thomas Highgate.

† † †

The Army Act, which was first introduced in 1881, was updated every year thereafter and passed as the Army (Annual) Act by Parliament, thereby enabling the government to maintain a standing army. The Army Act of 1881 formed part of the law of England, with one difference being that it was administered by military officers and court, and emphasised that 'in all times and in all places, the conduct of officers and soldiers as such is regulated by military law.'

As an example of the differences between civilian and military law in 1914–18, consider the situation of a factory worker who, if found asleep, could face dismissal in the worst case scenario, while a sentry found asleep in the front line could well have faced the death penalty. Although the circumstances are somewhat different, nevertheless the example highlights quite starkly the contrast in outcomes, particularly as a civilian falling asleep at their job commits no criminal offence, but under military law a soldier does.

Julian Putkowski, co-author of *Shot at Dawn*, was quoted in the *Independent* newspaper (27 May 1997) saying that his view of military executions was that they were designed to 'intimidate and frighten soldiers in the battlefield to get them to take part in pointless exercises in which thousands were slaughtered'.

† † †

The Army Act set out the following capital offences whilst on active service, which military law defined as 'whenever a person forms part of a force (1) engaged in operations against the enemy; (2) engaged in military operations in a country wholly or partly occupied by the enemy; or (3) in military occupation of any foreign country':

- Shamefully abandoning or surrendering a garrison, place or post to the enemy, or compelling another soldier to do so.
- Shamefully casting away their arms, ammunition or tools in the presence of the enemy.
- Treacherously corresponding with the enemy or through cowardice sending a flag of truce to him.
- Supplying the enemy with arms or ammunition or shielding an enemy who was not a prisoner.
- Taking service with the enemy having been made a prisoner.
- Knowingly while on active service, committing any act calculated to imperil the success of His Majesty's forces or any part thereof.
- Behaving in a cowardly manner or inducing others to behave like cowards.
- Leaving his commanding officer in search of plunder.
- Leaving a post or patrol without orders.
- Breaking into a military store.
- Forcing an entry past a sentry or striking a sentry.
- Impeding the Provost Marshal and his military police or refusing to assist them when called upon.

- Attacking anyone bringing up supplies or damaging property of the country in which he was serving.
- Deliberately discharging firearms, drawing swords, beating drums, making signals, using words, or by any means whatever to give a false alarm.
- Housebreaking for plundering purposes.
- Treacherously giving passwords to unauthorized people.
- Diverting, to his own unit, supplies meant for other formations.
- Being asleep or drunk on sentry duty or leaving a sentry post without being properly relieved.
- Disobeying an order from an officer on duty or striking or threatening an officer on duty.

The vast majority of the men executed had been found guilty of desertion because the possible alternative offence of cowardice would have been much harder to prove. Military Law defines desertion as 'absence without leave with the intention of permanently quitting the Service, or of evading a particular important duty, such as embarkation or going out in aid of the Civil Power'.

It is also necessary to understand a further and important difference between civilian and military courts. Civilian criminal courts are adversarial, with prosecution counsel pitted against defence counsel in an effort to prove guilt beyond reasonable doubt, and it is the legal teams that decide who gets called as a witness. A judge at the Old Bailey therefore cannot decide to summon a particular witness on the grounds that he or she might think such testimony would help establish guilt or innocence. In contrast, military courts are inquisitorial, in that they set out to establish what happened and as a result the court itself can summon and question any witnesses it considers necessary in the furtherance of that aim. Lastly, and so importantly, unlike in civilian criminal law, there was no right of appeal for those condemned to death by the military.

✝ ✝ ✝

The Army Act was enshrined in the *Manual of Military Law* in order to provide a framework that was universally consistent and predictable, and which set out the concepts of discipline in an accepted set of rules to control and order the army's activities, and to regulate the conduct of its members. Corrigan (2004) makes the point that, 'The only difference between an army and an armed rabble is discipline.' Army discipline comes from training, and then more training, backed up by a set of rules enshrined in military law, ignorance of which, as in civilian law, does not form an acceptable defence.

The types of punishments meted out to soldiers in the First World War are quite likely to be familiar to those who have read Bernard Cornwell's Sharpe novels, which are based on the Napoleonic Wars. Minor matters, such as being unshaven, not saluting a senior officer correctly, or having dirty equipment, were usually dealt with by the non-commissioned officers. Punishments would range from extra fatigues, extra exercise, the offender's confinement to barracks, or the loss of a day's pay. Such offences were generally irritating for all concerned, as were the punishments.

The rules for field punishment were set out in section 44 of the Army Act, and a man could be sentenced to no more than three months by a court martial or twenty-eight days by his commanding officer.

Field Punishment No.1 involved the offending soldier being bound or handcuffed to stop him escaping, and the rules allowed for the prisoner to be attached to a fixed object – without specifying what constituted a fixed object. In practice this led to prisoners being tied to the wheels of a gun carriage as if crucified, for no more than two hours a day, split between morning and afternoon, and for no more than three out of four consecutive days and for no more than twenty-one days in total. This form of punishment was not abandoned by the army until quite late in the war. Unsurprisingly, this form of punishment was very unpopular, not least when it was done in full view of the local population.

Albert Marshall, of the Essex Yeomanry, who was believed to be the last surviving First World War veteran to have fought on horseback, recalled guarding (Taylor-Whiffen, 2003):

> … a chap who had been tied to a wheel, without food or water, as a punishment for something. I can't remember what he'd done. But I felt sorry for him so I put my fag up to his lips so he could have a smoke. It was a very risky thing to do because if anyone had seen me they'd have tied me to the wheel as well!
>
> Years later I was walking down Oxford Street in London and I saw him. He recognised me immediately and thanked me. He said he'd never forgotten that fag.

The treatment of this soldier was despite military law specifically stating that punishment:

> …should not be inflicted in such a manner as is calculated to cause injury or to leave any permanent mark on the offender; and a portion of a field punishment must be discontinued upon a report by a responsible medical officer that the continuance of that portion would be prejudicial to the offender's health.

Archie Baxter (2014) was a conscientious objector who had served with the New Zealand Army, and recalled what Field Punishment No.1 felt like:

> My hands were taken round behind the pole, tied together and pulled well up, straining and cramping the muscles and forcing them into an unnatural position. The slope of the pole brought me into a hanging position, causing a large part of my weight to come on my arms, and I could get no proper grip with my feet on the ground, as it was worn away around the pole and my toes were consequently much lower than my heels. I was strained so tightly up against the post that I was unable to move body or limbs a fraction of

an inch. The pain grew steadily worse until by the end of half an hour it seemed absolutely unendurable.

Many officers supported the use of Field Punishment No.1 because they felt that it did at least provide an alternative to what would otherwise be a death sentence. By the end of the war some 60,000 men had been subjected to Field Punishment No.1 (Paxman, 2013). Sir Douglas Haig supported the use of Field Punishment No.1 on the grounds that it was an alternative to imprisonment. In his view, imprisonment would be an attractive alternative to the trenches for men of weak moral fibre, and such men needed to fear punishment, adding the justification that otherwise the 'recourse to the death penalty would be more frequent'. (Sheffield, 2012)

Field Punishment No.2 involved the offender being turned out in a full pack to be drilled, mostly at the double, sometimes by a military police sergeant, and possibly when the man or men concerned had just come out of the line. Another soldier (Van Emden, 2002) was given three weeks of Field Punishment No. 2, which meant that when off duty he had to spend his time emptying the latrine buckets. Later in the book there will be further examples of how prisoners and offenders were further punished by being involved in executions.

† † †

In addition to the Army Act and the *Manual of Military Law*, there were also the King's Regulations for the Army. All officers were required to study and know these, as they regulated all aspects of military life in a very detailed way. Every soldier would also be clearly told what the capital offences were and the punishment they could expect, when sections of the Army Act were read out on parade, and, in addition, each was given on enlistment an abbreviated, printed version of the capital offences to be kept in their pay book.

When a death sentence had been confirmed, the execution was carried out by the authority of the Army Act. Contained

As commander-in-chief, it was Field Marshal Haig's signature on the death
warrants; of the 302 men executed, just over 250 were on his watch. Haig's
post-war popular image as a ruthless disciplinarian was not one recognised by most
under his command.

within this very detailed document is information on the con-
stitution and conduct of a court martial, although it contains
nothing about the organisation of the act of execution itself.
So on what basis were the executions organised? How, for
example, was the number of men that made up a firing squad
determined, together with the distance they were to stand
from the condemned, and whether the condemned should be
tied to a stake or made to sit in a chair?

The *Manual of Military Law* and Army Acts 1881 and 1907, in regard to the death penalty, mention only that the conducting officer needed to apply to the Army Council for directions. This is repeated in the *Manual of Military Law* of 1914, where paragraph 100 states:

> An officer who confirms a sentence is responsible for seeing that the sentence is carried into effect, and for this purpose he will, where necessary, obtain the approval above required for a sentence of death and in all cases will give the necessary directions for the execution of the sentence.

The conclusion to be drawn from this is that the Army Act, the *Manual of Military Law* and the King's Regulations for the Army did not provide any form of standard operating procedure to cover military executions. Some research by the Royal Military Police Museum has established that there was also nothing included in the *Regulations for the use of the Provost Marshal's Branch, British Armies in France 1917* (2nd edition).

† † †

Nevertheless, some form of standard operating procedure did appear to exist because Fiennes (2012) reproduced the notes given to his grandfather Edward Montmorency Guilford in December 1917. Guilford was an Anglican chaplain with the 52nd Oxford and Buckinghamshire Light Infantry on the Western Front when he was ordered to attend the execution of Private Joseph Bateman, of the 2nd South Staffordshire Regiment, which took place on 3 December 1917. The notes were a carbon copy, covering no more than a couple of typed pages, which, although a little torn and ragged, were intact and still readable.

These notes were issued as a guide to the arrangements that needed to be made when a death sentence was to be carried out, so that it could be performed as quickly and as humanely as possible, and those parts of the orders relevant to this book are reproduced here:

Confidential

Execution of Sentence of Death by Shooting.

These notes are issued as a guide to all concerned when arrangements have to be made for carrying out a death sentence.

The main object to be effected is to carry out the sentence as rapidly and as humanely as possible.

Site

Select a site for the execution with a place of confinement alongside. The site should afford privacy and there must be some form of stop butt.

Time

Settle day and hour of execution. APM (Assistant Provost Marshal) to inform Divisional Headquarters. The best time for execution is just before daylight, but if this is not feasible, it can be carried out just before dusk.

Prisoner to be handed over to a guard of his own unit. The NCO (Non-commissioned Officer) in command of the guard to be of full rank and to be specially selected. He will receive instructions from the APM.

Promulgation to prisoner

The proceedings will be sent by Divisional Headquarters to the unit and the sentence will be promulgated by an officer of the unit to the prisoner about 12 hours previous to the execution. This should be done on arrival at the place of confinement. The proceedings of the FGCM (Field General Court Martial) will be handed over to the APM.

Chaplain

Ascertain the prisoner's denomination and arrange for services of a Chaplain. The Chaplain will attend the promulgation of the sentence to the prisoner and will inform the latter when it will be carried out. He may remain with the prisoner up to the time the latter is prepared for execution (ie when the APM enters the place of confinement and demands the prisoner from the guard) and will not be allowed further intercourse with him after that time. He may attend the execution and he will afterwards read the burial service. It is undesirable that he should wear vestments.

Medical Officer
Arrange with the Assistant Director Medical Services for the presence of a Medical Officer at the execution.

Grave and Digging Party
To be arranged by unit and will normally be in a recognised burial ground, but if this is not possible it will be chosen near the site for execution and in this case will be concealed from view of the prisoner as he approaches the spot. Digging party to be provided by the unit. The men will not be allowed to loiter near during the execution.

Post and rope
A wooden or iron post firmly fixed in the ground or a staple in a wall should be provided and a rope for tying the prisoner thereto.

Military Police
Military Police will be employed to prevent traffic from passing by the place of execution for half an hour before the hour fixed for execution and until all traces of its having taken place have been removed.

Firing Party
To consist of an Officer, 1 Sergeant and 10 men of the prisoner's unit. The sergeant will not fire. The Officer will be present at the promulgation of the sentence to the prisoner and will on that occasion receive from the APM any instructions as necessary. He will previously instruct the firing party as to their duties, impressing on them that the most merciful action to the prisoner is to shoot straight.

Procedure

The APM is responsible for all arrangements and for seeing the sentence carried out.

After promulgation, the prisoner should be allowed anything he wishes to eat, drink or smoke within reason. He will also be provided with writing materials if desired.

When being prepared for execution the prisoner will be identified by the NCO in charge of the guard in the presence of the APM and Medical Officer. The APM will collect pay book and identification disc and make them over to the NCO in charge of the guard for delivery at the unit's Orderly Room.

The prisoner will be handcuffed or have his wrists bound before being taken to the place of execution.

The Medical Officer will provide a three cornered bandage for blindfolding and a small paper disc for fixing over the heart. He will adjust these when requested by the APM.

He will also arrange for a stretcher in case the prisoner is unable to walk.

Firing party

Rifles will be loaded by the Officer i/c Firing Party and will be placed on the ground. One rifle will be loaded with a blank. Safety catches will be placed at safety. Distance from post 5 paces. The Officer will bring with him a loaded revolver.

The firing party will be marched into position by the APM whilst the prisoner is being tied to the post. The APM will so time this that the firing party will be ready for action simultaneously with the completion of the tying up.

The firing party will march in two ranks, halt on the rifles, turn to the right or left, pick up the rifles and come to a ready position, front rank kneeling, rear rank standing. They will press forward safety catch and come to the 'present' on a signal from the APM. The Officer, when he sees all the men are steady, will give the word 'fire'. This is to be the only word of command given after the prisoner leaves the place of confinement.

When the firing party has fired, it will be turned about and marched away at once by the Sergeant, the Officer remaining behind.

The Medical Officer will go forward and examine the body. If he considers that life is not extinct he will summon the Officer i/c of the firing party, who will complete the sentence with his revolver.

The Medical Officer will certify death and sign the death certificate which he will hand to the APM.

Removal of body
When death has been certified, the body will be unbound and removed to the grave under arrangements previously made by the unit.

The notes make it clear that from the time a death sentence has been passed on a man, he would be handed into the custody of the APM of the division, who would be in charge of making all the necessary arrangements and liaising with the prisoner's commanding officer, as necessary, once he was in receipt of all the formal paperwork from divisional headquarters.

The origins of these notes remain a stubborn mystery. The earliest documentation that the Royal Military Police Museum has concerning military executions is the *Provost Training in Peace and War, being the Manual of the Corps of Royal Military Police 1950* (pp. 213–15), which sets out a procedure that very closely accords to those issued to Guilford in 1917 – which is interesting in itself, as the death penalty was virtually abolished in the military in 1930, as will be discussed later.

The overall impression left by the notes given to Guilford is that they are very detailed and read as if based on the accumulation of good practice to date, although the source of the good practice and whether it applied across the whole British Army has not been possible to determine at the time of writing.

It is not clear why these notes were given to the chaplain and not to the APM, who had responsibility for the conduct of the execution. The likeliest explanation, particularly as Guilford was handed a carbon copy, is that the notes were given to him by the senior chaplain as a copy for his information about what was to happen so that he was forewarned and prepared – the equivalent of copying someone in on an email, for example.

In addition, although some of its phraseology might appear to be unmilitary in terms of its structure and language, Peter Fiennes has confirmed that although torn and a little ragged, it was in all other respects intact.

Instructions do exist for the execution of Private John Skone, of the 2nd Welch Regiment, on 10 May 1918, who was found guilty of the murder of Lance-Sergeant Edwin Williams on 13 April 1918. These were sent by Major Joseph Wesley, the deputy assistant adjutant-general, to Brigadier-General Morant, and are much briefer although essentially covering the same points as those issued to Guilford (Putkowski and Dunning, 2012). There is also a tantalising report of the experiences of Lieutenant-Colonel H. Meyler (Moore, 1999) which indicates that such regulations may have existed. Meyler recalled an execution in 1915 where he had detailed a firing squad from 'A' Company to shoot a man from 'B' Company, and went on to say, 'You may say that regulations do not allow this to be done. I have seen it done myself.'

Therefore, despite the concerns raised in the previous paragraph and in the absence of alternative documentation, the Guilford notes will be used as the basis for examining the roles and experiences of those who played a part in the executions.

Soldiers who had been executed were later buried in the same cemeteries as their comrades who had died in action. In September 1916, the adjutant-general issued an order which read:

> There is no rule that any man who has suffered the extreme penalty of the law should be buried near the place of execution. Any man who suffers the extreme penalty of the law may be buried in a cemetery, the inscription being marked DIED instead of KILLED IN ACTION or DIED OF WOUNDS.

† † †

Having taken into account the standards of the time, there are two major areas of concern: namely, the lack of a right to an appeal and the part played by chance. The right to an appeal is enshrined in British civilian law, so why did the politicians, presumably under pressure from the British Army hierarchy, agree to the removal of this right under military law? The simplest explanation is likely to be that it was because the offences were committed whilst on active service, and the army wanted to avoid having resources tied up in dealing with what could potentially be large numbers of appeals. This seems to fall under the term 'exigencies of the service', which seems to give approval for doing less than would normally be acceptable as circumstances demanded.

It seems an unavoidable conclusion that chance played too big a part in whether a death sentence was confirmed and carried out, and yet that did not seem to trouble the military hierarchy or the politicians of the day. If a soldier subject to military law was found guilty of an offence committed on active service that was subject to a mandatory death sentence, then in the absence of any mitigation, that should have been the sentence. It should not be used as a tool to correct perceived deficiencies in the discipline and fighting abilities of a battalion or regiment as this introduces a worrying level of subjectivity into the proceedings – as seems to be the case with Sir Douglas Haig's decision-making criteria, based on the limited number of diary entries that he made, which were both troublingly subjective and opaque. If Sir Douglas Haig, for example, considered that someone needed to be made an example of because 'The state of discipline in this battalion is not very satisfactory…', then, in his mind, a condemned soldier was expendable in the cause of making that example.

In the case of Private Arthur Earp, of the 1/5th Royal Warwickshire Regiment, who was executed on 22 July 1916 for the offence of quitting his post, Haig's attitude to capital punishment and the expendability of an individual soldier was

8th Lpools	In confinement awaiting Trial 24 days.			
	Tried by. F.G.C.M. at			22.10.76
	Ypres, for "When on Active			
	Service" deserting His			
1/8th 01810	Majesty's Service.			
No41/16	Finding; Guilty			
	Sentence; Death			
	Confirmation C.in.Chi			
	British Armies in the Field			
	The Sentence was duly			
	carried out at 6-16 a.m			2.11.16

Private Bernard McGeehan was shot for desertion at 6.16 a.m. on 2 November 1916. He was almost certainly autistic: 'Ever since I have joined up the men have made fun of me … Every time I go into the trenches they throw stones at me and say it is shrapnel and they call me all sorts of names. I have been out here 18 months and have had no leave.'

made clear. It had been recognised by the court martial and those in the chain of command that Private Earp had been 'unnerved by a barrage' and so, at each level, a recommendation for clemency had been supported – with the exception of General Gough, his army commander, and Haig as the commander-in-chief. Haig's practice was simply to write 'confirmed' together with his signature on the paperwork of those sentenced to death. However, in Private Earp's case, he wrote, 'How can we ever win if this plea is allowed?'

Almost certainly, Private Earp was suffering from shell shock and Haig was clearly concerned that any clemency shown would legitimise the condition and open the gates to a flood of similar cases as men sought to escape the trenches (Sheffield, 2012). It is clear, therefore, that Earp was shot purely and simply because he had shell shock and to discourage others from using it as an excuse for avoiding what Haig saw as their duty.

Such attitudes pre-dated Haig: in 1915, General Sir Horace Smith-Dorrien, commander of the Second Army, wrote to the

General Sir Horace Smith-Dorrien. 'There is a serious prevalence of desertion to avoid duty in the trenches, especially in the 8th Brigade and I am sure the only way to stop it is to carry out some death sentences.'

officers of the court martial convened to consider the case of Fusilier Joseph Byers, 1st Royal Scots Fusiliers: '… would urge that discipline in the 1st Battalion Royal Scots Fusiliers had been bad for some time past, and that a severe example is very much wanted.'

The impression that life was cheap and of no value beyond the needs of the army is one that, 100 years later, gives pause for thought, but in 1914–18 it would not have seemed so surprising. This is also a point that other military historians dispute, arguing that the officers and their men developed strong bonds, but, while this might have been the case at battalion level, those bonds would have been weaker the further up the command chain that decisions were being made, when the individuality of the person was replaced by a collective view.

This raises a further interesting point because, if a battalion was underperforming and this had been in some way drawn to the commander-in-chief's attention, then the battalion as a whole bore a collective responsibility if the sentence was confirmed. There is no evidence to suggest that this was ever acknowledged, but we will discuss later the impact that death sentences had within battalions and regiments.

The Irish Government Report (2004) gave other examples of the part played by chance and the collective responsibility of a condemned man's comrades:

> There have been far too many cases already of desertion in this Battalion. An example is needed as there are many men in the Battalion who never wished to be soldiers.
>
> I consider that, in the interests of discipline, the sentence as awarded should be carried out.
>
> [I recommend] the extreme example be carried out as a deterrent to other men committing a similar offence.
>
> The state of discipline of the unit as a whole is good, but there are individuals (such as the accused) in the unit who take advantage of leniency and for whom an example is needed.
>
> Under ordinary circumstances I would have hesitated to recommend the capital sentence awarded be put into effect as a plea of guilty has been erroneously accepted by the court, but the condition of discipline in the Battalion is such as to render an exemplary punishment highly desirable and I therefore hope that the Commander in Chief will see fit to approve the sentence of death in this instance.

† † †

The Army Acts, the *Manual of Military Law* and the King's Regulations are very detailed documents, but they have surprisingly little to say where the death sentence is concerned once the regulations for the conduct of court martial have been dealt with. The document that could be considered the closest thing to a standard operating procedure are the notes given to the Anglican chaplain Edward Guilford, and yet so far it has not been possible to establish their origins or how widely they were disseminated.

It has sometimes seemed within the published material concerning executions that the fact that 90 per cent of sentences were commuted was seen as something to be proud of, as a demonstration that somehow the system worked – yet really the opposite is true, even allowing for the fact that some of those sentenced were in fact serial offenders. If the British Army and the politicians were convinced of the need for the death penalty on active service then the sentence should have been mandatory with a right to an appeal. The British Army's apparent lack of transparency and honest conviction about the death sentence is also of concern, as evidenced by the practice of 'weeding out', or what is now known as redacting, to 'defeat the inquisitive', and the next chapter will deal with this aspect in more depth.

After the war, Mr H.V. Clarke (Corns and Hughes-Wilson, 2001), who stated that he had worked at General Headquarters (GHQ), the overall headquarters of the British Expeditionary Force, made what seems to be an extraordinary claim. He said that during his time at GHQ he had extracted data from the routine orders relating to executions which showed that the number of actual executions exceeded the official figures, and he wrote to newspapers stating that in his view the true number of executions was in fact 37,905.

Although no newspaper published his extraordinary claim, it came to the attention of the authorities, leading Clarke to state that he had, as a result, destroyed his evidence. Subsequently no evidence has ever been found to substantiate Clarke's claim and it is hard to believe (or maybe it's a case of not wanting to believe) that his claim of 37,905 executed men was accurate. After all, the figure he claimed was nearly twice the number killed on the first day of the Somme in July 1916, or the equivalent of thirty-seven wartime battalions – executions on that scale would have been hard to conceal from the soldiers, the public and the politicians. It was not something that the death-penalty abolitionist, Ernest Thurtle, ever raised during his long campaign. Also, an attrition rate at that level would have caused a shortage of men that the generals would have been keen to avoid, even allowing for their support of the death penalty. This would have broken one of the underlying tenets of the death penalty – that it should not contribute to a shortage of men.

But a final, and perhaps uncomfortable, thought before leaving this point, is the possible connection between Clarke's claim and the army's practice of weeding out problematic documentation. In 1917, the Under Secretary of State for War was asked in Parliament to discontinue the practice of naming soldiers who had been executed in routine orders, but he refused on the grounds that this would remove the deterrent nature of the sentence. These routine orders are notable for their absence from the official documents held today at The National Archives.

Army discipline was based on the ideas of intimidation and fear, but if these were not regulated then it should not be a surprise to see this leading to abuse. Military law is quite explicit about what could and could not be done where field punishment was concerned, and yet this chapter has outlined instances of abuse, and more will be discussed over the coming chapters. Is it really too big a step to say that if the regulations for field punishments were abused, then it should not be a surprise to find that the ultimate sanction, the sentence of being shot at dawn, was equally open to abuse in the way that it was organised?

† † †

We will now move beyond the discussion of the legal and organisational aspects of the executions to consider the individuals who found themselves cast as players in these very human dramas, and what their experiences can add to our understanding of this aspect of the First World War.

2

THE SELECTION OF
THE FIRING SQUAD

In the First World War men joined the army for many reasons, such as patriotism, thirst for adventure and wanting to do their bit with their mates. Even those who were conscripted would, to some extent, have shared those feelings, even in the face of increasing casualty lists and a growing awareness of what this war actually entailed. Somewhere in that mixture of feelings would have been an acceptance that war involved killing your enemy, but none would have thought as they headed for the Western Front that they might one day be called upon to kill one of their own.

To give this issue some perspective, a look at the figures involved shows that, given the number of men who were executed, the number of those involved in a firing squad or in some other role at an execution, would in turn have been small bearing in mind the fact that over 5 million British and Commonwealth soldiers served on the Western Front at some point in the First World War.

† † †

According to the notes given to Guilford, the firing squad was to 'consist of an Officer, 1 Sergeant and 10 men of the prisoner's unit'. Contrary to what the notes suggest, however, the firing squad was not always drawn from the condemned man's own unit, or indeed comprised the number of men specified.

The order to form a firing party produced different responses from the officers concerned. Some were sensitive enough to realise that being a member of a firing squad was not a universally popular duty. Those officers would therefore first of all ask for volunteers, possibly even offering bribes in the form of extra pay, leave or rum rations. If bribery did not work, then an officer might turn to those men who had been convicted of committing minor offences and yet still remained with the unit.

† † †

Ernest Thurtle, MP, was a leading member of the abolitionist movement seeking to end the death penalty in the military in the years after the First World War. In a general debate in the House of Commons in 1926 that sought the abolition of the death penalty, he made a specific attack on sentencing soldiers to death for sleeping at their posts. He maintained that sleeping at one's post was not a real, wilful act, adding that after the Commons had been sitting for sixteen hours, 'members all around fell asleep. If the House was kept up for ninety-six hours without any sleep at all he would guarantee that 75 or 80 per cent of the members would be falling into deep slumbers.'

Although the War Office denied Ernest Thurtle (amongst others) access to the records of those executed, he did manage to gather some evidence from those who had been involved in military executions in the First World War. A number of individuals wrote letters to Thurtle with their experiences; when these were published, he withheld the names of both the authors and of those shot. Subsequently, however, as more information has entered the public domain, it is now possible to reinsert some of the names concerned.

Thurtle (2013) included an extract from a previously published article written by a soldier by the name of Private Albert

Rochester, who had been sentenced to field punishment No.2 for an undisclosed offence. He had found himself taken by a military police corporal to a Royal Engineers depot where he was issued with three posts, three ropes and a spade, which he had to carry to a secluded spot. He was ordered to dig three holes, a specified distance apart, for the stakes, while all the time becoming more aware of their purpose.

The preparations were for the executions of three men from the 19th Durham Light Infantry on 18 January 1917. Lance-Sergeant Joseph Stones had been sentenced for 'casting away his arms', while Lance-Corporals Peter Goggins and John McDonald had been sentenced for quitting their post.

An article in the *Guardian* newspaper on 16 August 2006 carried a description by Private Albert Rochester of what he had witnessed:

> A motor ambulance arrives carrying the doomed men. Manacled and blindfolded, they are helped out and tied up to the stakes. Over each man's heart is placed an envelope. At the sign of command, the firing parties, 12 for each, align their rifles on the envelopes. The officer in charge holds his stick aloft and, as it falls, 36 bullets usher the souls of three of Kitchener's men to the great unknown.

Rochester went on to say:

> As a military prisoner, I helped clear the traces … I helped carry those bodies towards their last resting place. I took the belongings from the dead men's tunics … A few letters, a pipe, a photo. I could tell you of the silence of the military police after reading a letter from a little girl to 'Dear Daddy', of the blood-stained snow that horrified the French peasants, of the chaplain's confession that braver men he had never met than those three men he prayed with just before the fatal dawn. I could take you to the graves of the murdered.

On this occasion each of the condemned men was assigned a firing squad of twelve men. When the condemned men had been killed, Rochester was ordered to clear away all traces of what had taken place, collecting the blood-soaked straw from the foot of the posts and burning it, and removing the posts. All this, when his greatest fear that morning when summoned by the military police corporal, was that he was about to experience his first session of full pack drill!

This would then heap an extra level of punishment that would be out of all proportion to the original offences committed, as can be seen in a further letter discussed below, written to Ernest Thurtle, MP.

In letter No.4, its author, a sergeant in the 1st West Yorkshire Regiment, described being ordered to choose 'the two worst characters' in his platoon to form part of the firing squad for the execution of Lance-Corporal Alfred Atkinson, also of the 1st West Yorkshire Regiment, on 2 March 1915, for the offence of desertion. When the two men, who were acknowledged by the author to be tough men, returned, he wrote that they were sick, suffered from nightmares, and could not keep their food down. They said: 'The sight was horrible, made more so by the fact that we had shot one of our own men.'

A week later the same sergeant recalled how he was sergeant of the regimental guard, with thirty-two prisoners whom he described as 'mostly twenty-eight day men', when the execution of Private Ernest Kirk, 1st West Yorkshire Regiment, was ordered to take place on 6 March 1915. Some of the prisoners had been part of the previous firing squad and the order that the sergeant received made clear that: 'You must warn a party of twelve men from the prisoners you have (those who shot Lance-Corporal Alfred Atkinson must not be included).'

In his letter the sergeant went on to write about his experience of putting together that firing squad:

I witnessed a scene I shall never forget. Men I had known for years as clean, decent, self-respecting soldiers, whose only offence was an occasional military 'drunk' screamed

out, begging not to be made into murderers. They offered
me all they had if I would not take them for the job, and
finally when twelve of them found themselves outside
selected for the dreaded firing party, they called me all the
names that they could lay their tongues to. I remained with
the guard for three days, and I leave you to guess what I had
to put up with. I am poor with eight children, I would not
go through three more such sights for £1000.

The experience of these men is interesting because it would
appear from King's Regulations (K.R. 482) that:

> An offender in arrest or confinement is not to be required
> to perform any duty beyond handing over any cash, stores,
> or accounts for which he may be responsible, or fatigue
> orders on board ship, and he is not to bear arms except by
> order of his Commanding Officer, in an emergency or on
> the line of march.

†††

Private William Holmes of the 12th Battalion, London
Regiment, recalled an execution in 1917 of two soldiers where
the condemned were to be executed by members of their own
company and the composition of the firing squad was decided
by the drawing of lots:

> Those that were drawn out – four of them – knew what
> they had to do at 8 o'clock the next morning. They felt as
> I would have done; terrified, almost sick with the whole
> thought of it. They were going to go and shoot their own
> mates. But there you are, we had to have discipline.

There were occasions when the condemned man was viewed
by his peers as deserving to be shot and in this situation individuals may have been more willing to take part. Although
there might be personal sympathy for the man concerned, as

was the case with Private Holmes, such feelings were tempered on occasions by the view that there could be no excuse, as every soldier knew that they were going to fight and what the likely consequences of committing certain offences could be.

The majority, however, like Corporal Alan Bray (Arthur, 2002), had strong feelings that Englishmen should not be shooting other Englishmen, as they were in France to fight Germans. Bray wrote that in this instance he knew that the condemned man had lost his nerve to the extent that he could not have returned to the front line. In these cases personal sympathy was based upon shared service and experiences, friendship, and an understanding of the particular circumstances and issues faced by the individual concerned, leading them to conclude that the sentence was just not justified.

Private Stephen Graham (2009) has given an eye-witness account of the execution of Private Isaac Reid, of the 2nd Scots Guards on 9 April 1915. On this occasion, volunteers from the regiment had been asked to form the firing squad but none had been forthcoming, and so the battalion snipers were ordered to do it. Graham makes the comment that the lack of volunteers reflected the fact that nobody actually believed that Private Reid had disgraced the regiment.

Thurtle, in his letter No.5, includes an extract from an ex-private of the East Kent Regiment, who expressed his view that he should not have been part of the firing squad at the execution of a man whom he referred to as 'a chum of mine'.

† † †

Sometimes these approaches to raising a firing squad were not always successful, as Captain Stormont-Gibbs of the 4th Suffolks discovered when he received an order to form a firing party for the execution of Private Benjamin Hart of the 1/4th Suffolk Regiment on 6 February 1917, who had been sentenced for the offence of desertion:

I sent a chit to OC companies to supply a few men each
– wondering what would happen. As I expected everyone
refused to do it and I wasn't going to press the company
commanders on the subject. I rang up Brigade and had a
rather heated conversation about it and finally the poor chap
was shot by someone else – perhaps a well-fed APM …

It should be noted in passing that Hart had been a habitual
deserter, and knowing this, Stormont-Gibbs had made him his
servant to keep him out of the front line, but he had deserted
again and so this officer was being asked to form a firing squad
for someone that he would have known reasonably well.

Captain Slack, MC, of the 1/4th Battalion East Yorkshire
Regiment recalled in his memoirs an occasion in 1916 when
he had to select a subaltern and ten men to form a firing squad
(Macdonald, 1991):

I wasn't present at the execution. I didn't want to be.
Neither was it a nice job for the ten men. I consulted with
my Company Sergeant Major and he actually picked the
ten and I didn't go into details of how it was done, whether
the man was put in a chair or blindfolded, or anything, a
mark over heart – I didn't go into details at all. I didn't even
ask the subaltern afterwards what happened. It was a horrible thing to have to do, but it had to be done. It had no
effect on the men's morale.

This recollection reveals a number of interesting points as there
is a sense of 'out of sight means out of mind': Slack apparently
played no part in this process, as he left the company sergeant
major to select the men and did not seek to check the details
of the execution or provide any support to the subaltern either
before, during or after the event. It raises questions about the
basis on which the company sergeant major made his selection and whether or not this was fair – were names perhaps
placed in a hat and those whose names were pulled out were
the unlucky ones? Or did the decision involve favouritism or

the settling of scores? Slack was a brave man, as evidenced by his Military Cross, but does his handling of this situation reveal indifference, moral cowardice or someone who had at heart perhaps questioned the validity of military executions? And can it really be possible, given the experiences recounted in letter No.4, that the men concerned were left unaffected by their experience?

The most concerning aspect of what Captain Slack had to say about the condemned man was that 'he was a halfwit'. Slack went on to acknowledge that, at this stage of the war, the latest drafts of soldiers represented 'poor material', but even so, he does not argue against the death sentence, although he did write to the soldier's mother to inform her that her son had been killed in action.

† † †

Sometimes those charged with forming a firing squad resorted to subterfuge, as reported in Thurtle's letter No.1. On 26 September 1914, Private George Ward of the 1st Royal Berkshire Regiment was executed having been found guilty of cowardice. At the time, the men were out of the front line but were due to go back that night. The author of the letter takes up the story:

> To get the firing party ... they called for twelve men to carry tools. Now the men who carried tools at that time had the first chance of using them, so you see there were plenty of volunteers, but once on parade they quickly realised that their job was to shoot poor 'A'.

Captain M.L. Walkinton of the Machine Gun Corps wrote in his diary of his shock at being ordered by his colonel to form a firing squad from his company for the execution of Private Patrick Murphy, 47th Battalion, Machine Gun Corps, on 12 September 1918. Murphy had been convicted of desertion on three separate occasions. This was a firing squad of six long-service men, with one of them having a rifle loaded with a blank round – the significance of which will be discussed in the next chapter. Walkinton observes, 'although they all hated the job they loyally obeyed their orders.'

† † †

On 23 March 1916, Private F. Charles Bladen, of the 10th Yorks and Lancaster Regiment, was executed for the offence of desertion by a firing squad drawn from his own battalion. The execution detail was made up of the regimental sergeant major, the provost sergeant, an escort of one NCO, and two men, together with a firing squad that included the condemned man's platoon commander, Lieutenant A.W. Lamond, one sergeant and sixteen men, four of whom would have been the burial party. In this particular case very definite orders had been given that the men were not to be told in advance what they were about to be ordered to carry out, and the group was taken by bus to its billets close to the site of the execution.

Private Bladen was shot by a firing squad of twelve men, while Murphy, as discussed earlier, faced a firing squad of six men. There are other variations in the number of men who were in a firing squad and there is no evidence to suggest how these numbers were arrived at.

Captain T.H. Westmacott was the assistant provost marshal of the 1st Indian Cavalry Division and in order to gain instruction into the conduct of executions, he attended an execution on 14 April 1916 of Private Edward Bolton of the 1st Cheshire Regiment, who had been found guilty of desertion. Private Bolton was shot by a firing squad of twelve men, with six standing and six kneeling. He attended another execution on 21 July 1916 that had a firing squad of twenty-five men (five men from each squadron). On this occasion, although five bullets had gone through the disc pinned to the man's chest, the man still continued to breathe, and so Westmacott had to shoot him through the heart with his revolver to finish the affair.

Private Frank O'Neill of the 1st Sherwood Foresters was executed on 16 May 1915 by a firing squad of six men, only two of whom had a loaded rifle. Private William Scotton, 4th Middlesex Regiment, faced a firing squad of eight men on 3 February 1915, and the rest of his unit was ordered to witness his fate, while Private William Turpic, 2nd East Surrey Regiment, faced a firing squad of twelve men on 1 July 1915.

† † †

On occasions, soldiers at a base camp recovering from wounds that stopped them from fighting at the front – but which their officers thought did not preclude them from firing a rifle – were used to form a firing squad. To the pain and trauma of being wounded was then added the horror of shooting one of their own.

Sometimes an accused man would be taken to a military prison behind the lines where he would be tried. If convicted and the sentence was confirmed then it would be the responsibility of the prison commandant to provide a firing squad, in which case he might turn to the military police who guarded the prison or a military police unit nearby to provide a firing squad.

† † †

There is some anecdotal evidence that an order to form part of a firing squad was the only order that a soldier could refuse to obey, but it has not been possible to find any reference to this in the available regulations. In Arthur (2002), Corporal Bray talks of being warned that he was to be part of a firing squad to be detailed for the execution of Private Abraham Beverstein, of the 11th Middlesex Regiment, which was due to take place on 20 March 1916. That evening 'an old soldier … told me that it was the one thing in the Army that you could refuse to do. So I straightaway went back to the sergeant and said, "I'm sorry, but I'm not doing this", and heard no more about it.'

It is in all probability a myth and Bray was somehow lucky to have got away with it, because if refusal was an option why would anyone have taken part? Indeed, Private Kennedy (www.themanchesters.org) records a soldier voicing the view that they should not be asked to be a member of a firing squad and a staff officer replying:

> I can understand your feelings. I am aware that it is an unpleasant duty for all of you. It isn't pleasant for me either. But the responsibility is not yours. It lies elsewhere and you've got to obey orders. So I can make no exceptions. I'm afraid you will have to go through with it.

† † †

It only takes one bullet to kill a man, and yet from the evidence discussed above, firing squads could vary in number from two up to a staggering twenty-five men. There is very little evidence, therefore, that if Guilford's notes had been more widely disseminated they were being adhered to, though it is not clear who made the decision as to the size of the firing squad.

Various methods were used to form firing squads, ranging from chance through to the drawing of lots, asking for or bribing volunteers, or plain subterfuge. It does not seem in any way right that men should have been tricked into becoming part of a firing squad, but it happened. There does not seem to have been a set basis for selecting those to be in a firing squad and this, together with an abdication of responsibility by some officers to their sergeants, gave rise to opportunities for abuse in the form of favouritism, spite and the settling of scores.

More disturbing, though, is the thought that men, whose only offence had been to be found drunk, and who were typically subject to twenty-eight days' field punishment, were being ordered to form a firing squad. This seems to add an extra tier of punishment that is well outside what was laid down in military law.

Military law, as it applied in the First World War, makes it clear that any field punishment should not be inflicted in such a way as to leave any permanent mark on the offender. When this particular regulation was drafted, the permanent mark being referred to would have been physical, because it was later in the war that mental trauma was accepted by the military. Taking part in an execution as a member of a firing squad would have had a psychological effect on those involved, which was against military law, was unethical and which was out of all proportion to any offences the soldier may have committed.

It seems equally remarkable that men who were recovering from wounds but were not yet deemed fit enough to be returned to their battalion or regiment should have been considered fit enough to participate as a member of a firing squad. This seems to add a further level of trauma to men who had already been through so much. Even allowing for the standards and norms of the time, 100 years later this still seems callous, unethical and simply wrong.

Amongst their comrades there was indeed a degree of empathy for those sentenced to death, and in many cases undisguised sympathy based upon a greater understanding of what had driven a man to desert as a result of their shared service and experiences. It would, however, be wrong to claim that all soldiers, whilst they might empathise with the condemned man, automatically sympathised with them, because many were viewed as cowards who deserved nothing less than being shot. This was a point that was made in Parliament during a debate on First World War soldiers (Pardons) on 18 January 2006 by Keith Simpson, MP, who had interviewed, in his words, several hundred veterans (Hansard, 18 January 2006):

One question, among many others, that I invariably asked them concerned their attitude towards the men who were executed in the First World War for desertion, cowardice and so on. The survivors of that war had an ambivalent attitude towards those executions. That is borne out by the archives at the Imperial War Museum, whether oral or written. It was possible to find large numbers of men who, at the time and in their old age, regarded the executions as wrong, vindictive and not achieving their objective of deterring people from running away, but equally I found large numbers of veterans who were bitter. They might not necessarily condone the fact that ultimately the men were executed, but they were bitter that some men decided to abscond and, as they saw it, did not do their duty and let their muckers down. That is an equally balanced view.

While some officers might maintain that the morale of the men selected to form a firing squad remained unaffected, this view was not necessarily shared by the men themselves, and the next chapter will consider this further from the viewpoint of those in the firing squad.

3

THE FIRING SQUAD

A Royal Commission of 1949, which examined a variety of execution methods for their decency and humanity, concluded that the firing squad did not possess even the first requirement of efficiency – namely, the certainty of causing immediate death. Dr John Collees went further in an article in the *Observer* on 25 April 1995, writing, 'Dying from gunshot wounds effectively means bleeding to death, probably with the odd broken bone, and is therefore, only marginally preferable to stoning.'

The firing squad itself was in many ways recognised by the officers and the APM as the weakest part of the execution process, and often there were a number of bungled executions. There was always the possibility that members of the firing squad – whether from nerves, sympathy for the condemned or just poor marksmanship – would miss their target, with the unpleasant implication that the officer in charge would then have to finish the job off with a single revolver shot to the condemned man's head or heart. An example of this was the execution of Private Joseph Byers, of whom more will be mentioned later, which was witnessed by Margueritte Six, the daughter of the farmer on whose land it took place near Locre. The firing squad had already executed one man, Private Andrew Evans, but its first volley of the second execution was fired over Private Byers' head. Whatever the firing squad's motivation, a further volley was required. Piet Chielens, the curator of the Flanders Fields Museum in Ypres, attributed the firing squad's action to an unwillingness to shoot at Private Byers (Linklater, 1998).

It would have been surprising if the traumatic experience did not lead to members of the firing squad, and indeed the others present, suffering psychological stress, affecting their own ability to function afterwards. If the number of men who took part in a firing squad was small compared to the overall numbers serving, then it logically follows that very few, if any, commanding officers and other senior officers involved in confirming death sentences would themselves have witnessed such an event prior to the start of, and during, the First World War. As a result, they were asking soldiers and more junior officers to take part in something of which they themselves had had no first-hand experience, so therefore could not fully comprehend the effect that such involvement would have on a man's mental well-being. Perhaps this is not too surprising given that shell shock was not recognised until 1916 onwards.

Shell shock was believed to be the result of a physical impact on the brain caused by a shell landing nearby, although it could be generically used for a range of traumatic conditions. Men could be under enemy barrages for long periods of time and they would react in a number of ways. Lord Moran, who had served as a medical officer on the Western Front and was later to act as Sir Winston Churchill's personal physician, made the same point:

> Courage is will-power, whereof no man has an unlimited stock; and when in war it is used up, he is finished. A man's courage is his capital and he is always spending. The call on the bank may be only the daily drain of the front line or it may be a sudden draft which threatens to close the account.

Frank Richardson, in his postscript to Babington's book (2002), also wrote about the idea of a bank balance of courage which needs, from time to time, to be replenished. Each time this is required it will not only take longer to do, but will also not last as long – demonstrating that 'every soldier, however brave and resolute, has his breaking point' – and the point at which it all becomes too much would vary from person to person.

Good discipline and training helped many to withstand the mental strain involved without them seeming to reach their breaking point, but this could be undone by tiredness and adverse environmental conditions. Tolerance levels varied; some men, on reaching their breaking point, would go berserk and became a danger to themselves and to others, while others would become incoherent and unable to function in any way, even losing the ability to speak or to move. Others ran away from the source of the problem – although many soldiers were able to withstand the strain and function as normally as the circumstances allowed. As with many things in the First World War, luck played a large part in how such men were treated – was that soldier really ill, putting it on, or was he in fact a deserter? If he was unlucky and was viewed as a deserter, then he would be tried accordingly and would face the possibility of a death sentence. Others, after a short time out of the line, recovered sufficiently to be able to return, while others required hospitalisation – and it is here that class again rears its head as more officers were treated for shell shock than the other ranks.

An ex-sergeant of the 13th Middlesex Regiment, who had been in charge of a firing squad, wrote to Thurtle about a particular incident that he had experienced. On this occasion the firing squad was made up of ten men who had been selected from what he described as a few details left out of the line: they 'were nervous wrecks themselves', which leaves it open to conjecture as to whether their physical and mental condition was such that they were fit enough to undertake such a detail in the first place. The ex-sergeant wrote, 'two of them had not the nerve to fire. Of course they were tried (by court martial) but they were found to be medically unfit – their nerves had gone ...'

Private James Crozier of the 9th Royal Irish Rifles was just 16 years of age when he was executed on 27 February 1916. With feelings against this execution running high among his comrades, the APM and the military police had a very real fear that the firing squad would disobey the order to shoot. In his book *A Brass Hat in No Man's Land*, Brigadier-General Crozier (no relation) wrote about this particular execution and seemed to take some pride in the arrangements made for the shooting of a young man – a young man whom he had, in fact, recruited himself, and had assured the boy's distraught mother that he would personally keep an eye on her son. Where the feelings of the men were concerned, his attitude was more or less one of 'so what, they would just have to get on with it':

> There are some hooks on the post; we always do things thoroughly in the rifles. He is hooked on like dead meat in a butcher's shop. His eyes are bandaged … A volley rings out – a nervous volley it is true, yet a volley. Before the fatal shots are fired I had called the whole battalion to attention. There is a pause, I wait. I see the medical officer examining the victim. He makes a sign, the subaltern strides forward, a single shot rings out. Life is now extinct … We march back to breakfast while the men of a certain company pay the last tribute at the graveside of an unfortunate comrade. This is war.

Given that James had been known to Crozier (Putkowski and Sykes, 1996), this makes for quite difficult reading, but Crozier in his book never admits to having this more personal knowledge of James. Indeed, Crozier refers to the unfortunate private as Crocker, a name that does not appear in Putkowski and Sykes' list of the men executed in the First World War, which is included in their book as Appendix 2. Was Crozier being genuinely or deliberately forgetful in his book? It is difficult to believe that he had really forgotten James' surname. Was he still looking out for James' interest by seeking to protect his mother? This is possible given that he was perhaps laying a false trail and, in his own words, he had said that he

Brigadier-General Frank Crozier. This volatile Irish officer had a remarkable career. After the war he was made commandant of the Auxiliary Division, a paramilitary unit of the Royal Irish Constabulary at the height of the Troubles, and resigned in highly controversial circumstances. After being declared bankrupt for a second time, he was involved in the League of Nations Union and then turned to pacifism, becoming a founder member of the Peace Pledge Union. How much did this have to do with his involvement with executions during the war and after it?

did not want the family told, and so ordered the inclusion of Crozier/Crocker in the list of those killed in action. This would have enabled Mrs Crozier to receive any allowances due, but unfortunately this subterfuge did not ultimately work and she received nothing.

Even more disturbing would be the thought that he was attempting to deny prior personal knowledge of James and the fact that, as James' battalion commander, he did not recommend that his sentence should be commuted and instead recommended the death sentence. There is possibly some substance to this: why did he feel the need to keep up the pretence in a book written in 1937? By then Mrs Crozier knew James' fate and had already experienced the repercussions from her son being executed.

A further worrying aspect of this story is that at about the same time that Private Crozier deserted, a subaltern by the name of Rochdale (this could be Brigadier Crozier disguising the name of the officer concerned because in other documents he is named as Lieutenant Arthur Annandale) committed the same offence. Crozier considered that the officer's desertion was made worse by him having displayed cowardice in front of his men. Rochdale was charged and, much to Crozier's dismay, he learned that he 'was to be released from arrest and all consequences'. When it was suggested that Rochdale be returned to his battalion, Brigadier Crozier refused to accept Rochdale back, saying, 'the least said about this the better, except to remark that had justice been done according to our code, regrets would have been fewer than in the case of [Crozier].' Despite the blatant inequality of treatment right under his nose, Brigadier Crozier did not hesitate to recommend the death penalty for Private Crozier.

† † †

The notes given to Guilford set out the following instructions for the firing squad, and it is against these that the experiences of those involved will be discussed:

To consist of an Officer, 1 Sergeant and 10 men of the prisoner's unit. The sergeant will not fire. The Officer will be present at the promulgation of the sentence to the prisoner and will on that occasion receive from the APM any instructions as necessary. He will previously instruct the firing party as to their duties, impressing on them that the most merciful action to the prisoner is to shoot straight.

Rifles will be loaded by the Officer i/c Firing Party and will be placed on the ground. One rifle will be loaded with a blank. Safety catches will be placed at safety. Distance from post 5 paces. The Officer will bring with him a loaded revolver.

The firing party will be marched into position by the APM whilst the prisoner is being tied to the post. The APM will so time this that the firing party will be ready for action simultaneously with the completion of the tying up.

The firing party will march in two ranks, halt on the rifles, turn to the right or left, pick up the rifles and come to a ready position, front rank kneeling, rear rank standing. They will press forward safety catch and come to the 'present' on a signal from the APM. The Officer, when he sees all the men are steady, will give the word 'fire'. This is to be the only word of command given after the prisoner leaves the place of confinement.

When the firing party has fired, it will be turned about and marched away at once by the Sergeant, the Officer remaining behind.

† † †

Private William Holmes, of the 12th Battalion, London Regiment (Arthur, 2002), wrote of how he and his colleagues drew lots to determine the four who would make up the firing squad for two men who were to be executed for desertion. The four men were then organised into pairs, and were told that one of them had to fire at the head of their designated prisoner and the other at his heart. There is no suggestion in this case that any blank ammunition was used.

Arthur (2002) has included the extract from Holmes in his chapter for 1917, but these same recollections are also included in Lister (2013), where they in fact refer to the execution of a young soldier, Private Abraham Beverstein, of the 11th Middlesex Regiment, who had enlisted at the age of 18 under the assumed name of Harris, and was executed on 20 March 1916 when just 19. Beverstein enlisted under a false name because it was considered dishonourable in certain Jewish circles to be a soldier, and Harris is the name on his gravestone.

Private Beverstein had written to his mother on 2 July 1915 to tell her that he had been 'in the trenches four times and came out safe'. In January 1916, the Beverstein family received notification from the Infantry Record Office, dated 15 January, informing them that Private Beverstein 'was ill at 38th Field Ambulance, France, suffering from wounds and shock (mine explosion)'.

A couple of weeks later the family received a letter from Private Beverstein in which he wrote:

> Dear Mother, we were in the trenches and I was ill, so I went out and they took me and put me in prison, and I am in a bit of trouble now and won't get any money for a long time. I will have to go in front of a court. I will try my best to get out of it. But dear Mother, try to send some money. I will let you know in my next [letter] how I get on. Give my best love to Father and Kath.

The letter is interesting in many ways because it is not clear whether by his comment, 'I will try my best to get out of it', Private Beverstein knew that he faced the death penalty and was putting on a brave face for his family or whether he really was unaware of the seriousness of the situation he was in. If it was the former, then he was being very brave, but if it was the latter, then it demonstrates that two years after the start of the war the deterrent aspect of the penalty was not working.

In April 1916, the family was informed that Private Beverstein had been shot for desertion just weeks after being in a field hospital suffering from wounds and shock.

It is likely that the other soldier executed was Private Samuel McBride of the 2nd Royal Irish Rifles as he is the only other soldier listed in Corns and Hughes-Wilson who was executed on that date and, like Beverstein, he was also buried in the Sailly-Labourse Communal Cemetery.

Interestingly, for each man executed, the firing squad constituted just two men and not the number given in Guilford's notes above. Nearly 100 years later, we can only imagine what those four men felt both before and after the execution, given that there is no mention of blank ammunition, and each would have been aware, as would have been the APM and the officer in charge, of whether or not their bullets had found their target.

In 1916, the soldiers of the 18th Manchester Regiment were dismayed to be told that one of their comrades was to be shot for desertion, and on this occasion the firing squad consisted of six men, who were told by an equally unhappy officer (Moore): 'I only hope to God you shoot straight.'

On this occasion, those in the firing squad were separated from the rest of the regiment the night before the execution to receive their instructions. As a reward for the unpleasant task ahead of them, they were allowed to relax and enjoy a drink, although they would have been supervised to ensure that none drank enough to render themselves senseless and therefore unable to take part the next morning. The soldier, Private William Hunt, was executed on 14 November 1916 for the offence of desertion. Hunt was certified as dead by Lieutenant G.C. Robinson, RAMC.

On 23 March 1916, Private F. Charles Bladen was executed for the offence of desertion by a firing squad of twelve men drawn from his own battalion of the 10th York and Lancaster Regiment. On the eve of the execution, the entire firing squad was taken by bus some distance away from the rest of their regiment, under specific instructions that they should not be told of the task awaiting them.

† † †

As the war progressed, it became the accepted practice that at least one of the rifles, which were loaded usually by the APM and the officer in charge, was loaded with a blank cartridge. There are some orders concerning the execution of Private James Carr, of the 2nd Welch Regiment, who was executed for desertion on 7 February 1916, which state that 'the officer should personally load the rifles, 9 with ball and one unloaded or loaded with blank'.

In addition, some officers then mixed up the rifles. All this was done to help alleviate any feelings of guilt on the part of those in the firing squad, although it is now accepted that an experienced soldier would not have been fooled, as evidenced by Rifleman Henry Williamson (Arthur, 2002): 'We knew by the recoil if it was loaded with ball or not.'

Nevertheless, this practice did act as a palliative by allowing some of those compelled to be part of the firing squad to convince both themselves and others that whatever the strength of the recoil, they had not fired the fatal shot. An unintended consequence of this practice was that, as a result of the rifles being mixed up, those in the firing squad found themselves having to use a rifle that they were unused to, which did not lend itself to accurate shooting.

Babington (2002) summed this practice up well when he wrote: 'Right up to the moment of taking aim each member of the firing party could continue to hope that he alone might be absolved from playing a part in the killing of a comrade.'

† † †

One soldier, Corporal Alan Bray, recalled that while he was in the trenches he was told that he would be one of six men detailed to form a firing party to shoot four men from another battalion who had been accused of deserting. He said that this left him very worried because he did not think it right that Englishmen should be shooting other Englishmen, as he thought he was in France to fight the Germans. A further cause for concern was that he thought he understood why these particular men had deserted, given that they had been in the trenches without a break for several months under conditions that would affect any man, adding that consequently, he had no appetite for shooting them.

In letter No.2 that was sent to Ernest Thurtle, the author wrote about the execution, on 26 April 1916, of Private Henry Carter from the 11th Middlesex Regiment, who had been found guilty of desertion. He had deserted after six days and nights of continuous bombardment and was known by his comrades to be 'a bundle of nerves'. The condemned man had joined the army when just 17 years of age and was executed eighteen months later while still underage.

Letter No.5 is in a similar vein, as the writer makes plain that he considered Private William Scholes of the 2nd South Wales Borderers, who was executed on 10 August 1918 for desertion, to have been no coward and 'one of his best pals'.

Even more disturbing is the case of Private James Smith of the 1st Battalion of the Lancashire Fusiliers, who was found guilty of wilful disobedience and sentenced to death. According to his great-nephew Charles Sandbach (Warren, 2009), most of the firing squad who sympathised with Smith first of all refused to shoot the condemned man and, when forced to do so, deliberately missed the marker over his heart, leaving him wounded but alive. Incredibly, his friend, Private Richard Blundell, was then ordered to shoot him because the officer in charge, Lieutenant Collins, could not do it himself. This story was repeated in the House of Commons during an adjournment debate in 2009, the full text of which is included as Appendix 3, where additional detail about the case of Private James Smith can be found:

Early on the morning of 5 September, a small patrol of soldiers from Jimmy's own unit entered a barn at Kemmel Château in Belgium to clean their weapons prior to re-engagement with the enemy. They were told that, first, they had a special duty to perform, and they were taken outside into a courtyard where they found their friend, Jimmy

Smith, blindfolded and tied to an execution chair in front of a wall, with a white target pinned to his tunic, just above his heart. Protesting furiously to the commanding officer, the 12-man firing squad – 11 privates and a non-commissioned officer – was summarily ordered to execute Jimmy. The lads aimed and fired, the majority deliberately missing the target. However, Jimmy was wounded, the chair was knocked over and he lay writhing in agony on the ground.

The young officer in charge of the firing squad was shaking like a leaf, but he knew now that he had to finish Jimmy off by putting a bullet through his brain with his Webley pistol. He lost his nerve, however, and could not fire the pistol in his hand as Jimmy continued to writhe in agony on the ground.

One of Jimmy's friends, 23643 Private Richard Blundell, who hailed from Everton in Liverpool, was then ordered by the commanding officer to take the Webley pistol and kill Jimmy. Jimmy's death was recorded on that day at 5.51 am. The 12 members of the firing squad were given 10 days' leave after that tragic event in the heat of battle. That was unusual.

Private Blundell lived until he was 95 and carried the memory of that day with him until he died. He was heard to utter, when he was near to his own death, 'What a way to get leave.'

In an article in the *Boston Sunday Globe* (12 November 2000), a veteran by the name of John Laister recalled being part of a firing squad when he was a teenager, and when the time came for him to take aim he saw that the soldier he was about to shoot was younger than him: 'There were tears in his eyes and tears in mine.'

† † †

Victor Silvester is now known as a famous dance band leader, but in 1914 he was just a boy of nearly 15 years of age who had managed to enlist. His true age was only discovered in 1917 after he was wounded, and he was subsequently sent back to England. He was to claim shortly before his death in 1978 that he had taken part in the execution of five soldiers, because when recovering from his wounds at Étaples in 1917 he was detailed to act as a messenger for the commandant's office. A sharp-eyed officer saw the crossed-rifle badge on Silvester's sleeve, which denoted that he was a first-class marksman, and commented that he would be useful for what he described as 'special duties'. Silvester was subsequently to find out that this meant having to be a member of a firing squad, and he described one such occasion in graphic detail (Allison and Failey, 1986):

> The tears were rolling down my cheeks as he went on attempting to free himself from the ropes attaching him to the chair. I aimed blindly and when the gunsmoke had cleared away we were further horrified to see that, although wounded, the intended victim was still alive. Still blindfolded, he was attempting to make a run for it still strapped to the chair. The blood was running freely from a chest wound. An officer in charge stepped forward to put the finishing touch with a revolver held to the poor man's temple. He had only once cried out and that was when he shouted the one word mother. He could not have been much older than me. We were told later that he had in fact been suffering from shell-shock, a condition not recognised by the army at the time.

Silvester recalled the effects of taking part in an execution as disturbed sleep and physical illness, claiming that he had been hospitalised and strapped to a bed to stop him from deserting. There is, though, some doubt about his recollections, as Corns and Hughes-Wilson contend that his story bears no relation to the facts.

† † †

The condemned prisoner did not always meekly make his way, or allow himself to be easily led, to the stake or chair to be used in his execution, thereby creating further horrors for the firing squad, as was contained in Ernest Thurtle's letter No.1. This letter appears to refer to the death of Private George Ward, 1st Berkshire Regiment, who was executed on 26 September 1914. (The letter gives the date of the execution as 30 September 1914, but the list in Corns and Hughes-Wilson has no executions listed for that date, although Ward was from the 1st Berkshire Regiment so the details appear to match in all other respects.)

The men of the firing squad would already have been feeling somewhat aggrieved by the time Ward was brought to the place of execution, as they had been tricked into being the ones detailed, as was covered earlier in this chapter. Ward, though, was not about to cooperate, and broke free of the sergeant of the guard and ran off. The story is picked up in the letter: '…the firing party fired at him on the run, wounding him in the shoulder. They brought him back on a stretcher, and the sergeant of the guard was ordered by the Provost Marshal to finish him off as he lay wounded.'

To the horror of having to shoot one of their own was added the fact that they had not killed him outright and then had to watch him despatched by the sergeant.

† † †

Those involved in a firing squad had a variety of experiences. One soldier recalled being detailed to be part of a firing squad for the execution of a deserter. The prisoner on this occasion was dressed in a set of civilian clothes, and the men were told to shoot at a piece of white cloth pinned over his heart.

Another recalled a Sunday when the whole battalion was made to parade to witness the humiliation of Privates Beverstein and McBride, who had deserted and as a result were to be shot. The two men had their caps and all insignia removed, as part of the army's ritual humiliation of the

Firing squad in 1917.

Sylvia Pankhurst knew Mr and Mrs Beverstein and took up their son's case. She published his letters and protested against the injustice of executing a 19-year-old volunteer who had been in the trenches for eight months and had only just come out of hospital with injuries and shell shock. There was a question in the House of Commons about the case, but the only outcome was that from then on executed soldiers were simply said to have 'died of wounds'.

condemned, told they were to be shot next day, and that they were each to be shot by a pair of their comrades. There was sympathy in the platoon for the two men but even more sympathy for their parents, who were told only that their sons had been killed in action. The soldier added that every man took punishment as a fact of life, as they did death.

Private William Hunt, of the 18th Manchester Regiment, was executed on 14 November 1916 having been found guilty of desertion, and Private P.J. Kennedy, MM, later recalled that he and five others were detailed to form the firing squad. Once the sentence had been promulgated, Kennedy said that the military police took over control of the proceedings, and in an attempt to make the whole business easier for all concerned, they tried to ply the condemned man with alcohol in an attempt to get him drunk – but Hunt refused.

On the eve of the execution, the firing squad was marched to the designated site for the following morning's grim event. While the officers discussed various matters, the men were able to get their first sight of the 'heavy kitchen chair' that Hunt would be sat on. When the discussions between the officers were finished, the men were briefed and were then taken through a rehearsal, when their officer said, 'Right. Shall we try it now?'

Hunt was not cooperative the next morning and refused to walk to the stake, ensuring that his would not be an execution marked by quiet dignity as he was dragged into position. Hunt was not blindfolded, either as a result of further non-cooperation or because it was simply overlooked in the rush to get it over and done with.

The men's rifles were taken from them and loaded, one with a blank, and the officer urged them to aim carefully at Hunt, who would be sitting in a chair fewer than ten paces in front of them, as he did not want to have to finish matters off. But the emotion of the occasion got to the men and the officer was required to finish Hunt off with a revolver shot to the head. Maybe as a punishment for not doing their job properly, Kennedy and the others were then detailed to take down the body, clean up the area around the stake and then bury Hunt. When they removed Hunt's body from the chair, Kennedy recalled that one of the men noticed that the dead man's hair was 'standing up stiff and straight from sheer terror'. To add to their woes, they discovered on arrival at the cemetery near Bailleulment that no grave had been prepared. They then had to borrow some tools and dig the grave themselves, wrapping the body in a waterproof cape.

Private Kennedy, like many of his comrades, felt confused, as just eighteen months earlier they had received praise from Sir Douglas Haig, and now the battalion had a stain on its good name when the fact of the execution was publicised on parades and in routine orders.

The death of Private Hunt was reported in the *Manchester Evening News* on 30 November 1916. It said simply that he had died of his wounds.

† † †

Private Stephen Graham, of the Scots Guards, wrote a book in 1919 about his experiences on the Western Front, and included a description of an execution which is thought to be that of Private Isaac Reid. Graham's book starts with the sentence: 'The sterner the discipline the better the soldier, the better the army', which gives a clue as to his stance where executions were concerned.

Graham's battalion was ordered to parade around three sides of a square to witness this execution, and this necessitated the men getting up an hour earlier to put on their full fighting kit in the dark. Private Reid was in his 'walking out attire' and appeared relaxed and free to talk to his friends. Graham wrote that volunteers had been unsuccessfully called for to form the firing squad, which he saw as a sign that Reid was viewed as not having disgraced the regiment. As a result, Reid was to be shot by the battalion's ten snipers and Reid encouraged them, 'Don't miss. Fire through my heart.' Then, having lit a cigarette, he took up his place against the tree that had replaced the more traditional stake. Reid asked not to be blindfolded but his request was turned down. With that, the parade was brought to attention and the snipers took up their positions and a deadly volley ensued.

Perhaps wisely, the officers then had the men sent out on a long route march, which would have had the effect of burning off any anger that they may have had.

† † †

Faced with horror and bloodshed, some men noticed different things where executions were concerned, as was the case with Private Sidney Suffield, who had only just arrived on the Western Front when he was ordered to form part of a firing squad. The man to be executed was Private Frederick Slade of the 2/6th London Regiment. Private Slade had arrived on the Western Front in early 1917 and was a stretcher bearer. However, on 26 October 1917 he had refused to parade prior to the regiment moving up the line and was consequently arrested. At his court martial on 14 November 1917, Private Slade claimed mental incapacity due to his exposure to the horrors of the war, but this was refuted by a captain from the Royal Army Medical Corps, which effectively sealed his fate. He was executed for disobedience on 14 December 1917, and Private Suffield was struck by the way the execution was carried out in complete silence apart from the rifle volley fired by the firing squad.

† † †

Each firing squad had an officer in charge; this was a role that was usually undertaken by junior officers, and was summarised by Crozier (1937) in his usual blunt and forthright manner, when briefing a young subaltern:

'You will be in charge of the firing party … the men will be cold, nervous and excited. They may miss their mark.

You are to have your revolver ready, loaded and cocked; if the medical officer tells you that life is not extinct you are to walk up to the victim, place the muzzle of the revolver to his heart and press the trigger. Do you understand?' 'Yes Sir' came the quick reply. 'Right' I add, 'dine with me in the mess tonight!'

I wanted to keep this young fellow engaged under my supervision until late at night to minimise the chance of his flying to the bottle for support.

One cannot begin to imagine the young subaltern's feelings on hearing those words. Crozier, meanwhile, was intent on ensuring that the subaltern did not turn to alcohol, thereby rendering him unfit to command the firing squad. The young officer would undoubtedly have preferred to get drunk and take the consequences if he had known what he would have to do the next day – he did, in fact, have to complete the sentence on Private James Crozier as the firing squad had failed to do its job.

In the orders relating to the execution for desertion of Private William Roberts, of the 4th Royal Fusiliers on 29 May 1916, Captain H.H. Pridmore, on behalf of the brigadier-general commanding the 9th Infantry Brigade, states, 'Please choose your officer carefully.'

† † †

The notes given to Guilford outline three parts to the role of the officer in charge of the firing party: namely, loading the rifles, giving the order to fire and, where necessary, administering the coup de grace:

Rifles will be loaded by the Officer i/c Firing Party and will be placed on the ground. One rifle will be loaded with a blank. Safety catches will be placed at safety. Distance from post 5 paces. The Officer will bring with him a loaded revolver.

The Officer, when he sees all the men are steady, will give the word 'fire'. This is to be the only word of command given after the prisoner leaves the place of confinement.

The Medical Officer will go forward and examine the body. If he considers that life is not extinct he will summon the Officer i/c of the firing party, who will complete the sentence with his revolver.

† † †

To be present when one man was executed can be counted as a rarity, but Captain G. Macready had just joined the 8th Division as a staff officer in April 1915 when a few months later, due to the illness of the APM, he was ordered to officiate at the execution of five men. The executions of Private Bert Hartells, Private Alfred Thompson, Private Ernest Fellowes, Corporal Frederick Ives and Private John Robinson, all of the 3rd Worcestershire Regiment, took place on 26 July 1915, and all had been sentenced for desertion.

The notes to Guilford state that the officer in charge of the firing squad, when the moment came, was to 'give the word "fire"', and this should be the last word the condemned man ever heard. There were a number of silent variations on this which were thought to be more humane: namely, the lowering of the officer's sword or dropping a handkerchief, but of course those most affected by this were not in a position to supply feedback on the humanity of this action.

Once the volley rang out, the officer would then have to wait for the medical officer to check whether the men had fired accurately and the prisoner was dead. It is hard to imagine what was going through the officer's mind as he waited to hear whether he would be called upon to administer the coup de grâce. On one occasion, Winter writes, 'A man was shot for cowardice. The volley failed to kill. The officer in charge lost his nerve, turned to the APM and said, "Do your own bloody work, I cannot."'

The notes to Guilford state that 'one rifle will be loaded with a blank', but the practice again varied, from one rifle loaded with a blank to only one rifle loaded with live ammunition, and it is likely that a young officer would be guided in that practice by the more experienced APM.

The young officers who were placed in charge of the firing squad were not immune from feelings of sympathy for the condemned man themselves, but were just as powerless to do anything about it. On 9 March 1917 Private John Rogers of the 2nd Battalion of the South Lancashire Regiment was executed having been sentenced for desertion by a firing squad drawn from his comrades under the command of his second lieutenant I. W. F. Agabeg.

† † †

There is little doubt, therefore, that the firing squad was the weakest part of the process, which caused concern for the officers involved. Members of the firing squad, whether individually or collectively, could and did miss their target for a variety of reasons such as incompetence, nerves, unfamiliarity with their allotted rifle or sympathy for the condemned man. It is a matter for debate whether, in the event that you sympathised with the condemned man, it was preferable to miss your target, knowing that if wounded he would still be killed by the officer in charge, or to fire accurately and end their suffering.

Based on today's knowledge of mental trauma, it cannot be a surprise that those men who formed the firing squad would have been affected by what they were being ordered to do. The extent to which the men were affected could be subject to such factors as how they had been selected, their physical and mental condition at the time, and their feelings towards the condemned man, as well as being involved in the execution itself. It took time, though, for the military hierarchy to accept and to acknowledge that mental trauma and shell shock could affect the fighting man, as it even took the medical profession some time to accept this universally. In fairness, there were men who would do whatever was asked of them, and who just got on with it without any discernible effect at the time, though whether and how this might have manifested itself after the war is not known.

In a letter to the *Observer* newspaper on 11 November 2001, Mrs Anne Mary Jones urged that the men of the firing squads, like her father, should also not be forgotten, writing, 'They joined the army to shoot the enemy, not terrified boys and shell-shocked men. My father was one such and the experience remained the most dreadful thing he ever had to do.'

Despite this, the practice of loading one rifle with blank ammunition could be viewed as an acknowledgement of the potential mental and social impact of being detailed to take part in a firing squad, although, as previously mentioned, in reality the men would have known by the force of the recoil what type of ammunition they had just fired.

Whatever the standards and practices of the time, it does seem strange that the army had not laid down a precise number for the size of the firing squad, which seems to have varied from two up to twenty-five, although the majority do appear to have been closer to the figure stipulated in the note given to Guilford.

Whilst the members of the firing squad could draw some comfort from being only one of a number of men put in the situation of shooting a fellow British soldier – or convincing themselves, if they did not know already, that their rifle had been loaded with blank ammunition – there was no such solace for the invariably young subaltern in charge. They had to stand closer to the condemned man and, if required, would have to administer the coup de grâce, with no chance of arguing that they had fired a blank.

As Lewis-Stempel (2011) sets out in his book, many of the subalterns had enlisted straight from school and, given that the average time a junior officer survived was little more than six weeks, it is awful to think that for some, their time on the Western Front should have included the experience of being an officer in charge of a firing squad.

4

THE ARMY CHAPLAIN

Whichever side of the conflict they were on, the majority of both officers and men would have put their trust in their God to see them through the war at a time when societal norms meant that an individual had to choose whether to opt out of organised religion rather than to opt in, as is the case today. Few seemed to have questioned how the same God could operate on both sides of the line, perhaps because, for the majority, believing was enough without wondering why or how, but if such questions were raised then their army chaplains were on hand and would, with certainty, have been able to put their minds at rest.

Church parade on a Sunday was a compulsory event for all men, whatever their beliefs or faith. Chaplains from denominations other than Roman Catholic did not tend to go too near the front, leading some soldiers to feel that although they might give a fire-and-brimstone speech exhorting the troops to advance and fight, they did not share the inherent dangers involved. This is captured nicely in a quote from Siegfried Sassoon (Holmes, 2005), who was unhappy with a particular chaplain's choice of words. 'And now God go with you,' he had told a group of men bound for the front. 'I will go with you as far as the station.'

Perhaps in this individual's defence, it should be pointed out that Anglican chaplains were expressly instructed to stay away from the front line, although this situation changed in 1916, when they were incorporated into the forward field ambulances and main dressing stations. Julian Bickersteth, who became a senior Anglican chaplain in the 56th (London) Division and was awarded the Military Cross, felt it was important for his credibility with the men to go where they went, as he explained (Lewis-Stempel, 2011): 'I went out with a wiring party into no-man's land last Friday, got back at 4.00am – a most interesting experience. I was glad of it because I do so dislike the men to have to listen to someone who has not been with them under all conditions.'

Army chaplains, and there were some 3,500 chaplains serving with the British Army by November 1918 (Snape, 2004), were given officer rank and carried out a range of duties from administering to the dead and dying, performing burials, giving troops absolution as they went forward, attempting to maintain morale, and even on occasions censoring letters from the front. Snape makes the point that from January 1916 onwards, part of the chaplains' role was to raise morale and foster discipline amongst the troops and, therefore, it could be argued that the continued execution of offenders after that date represented failure on their part.

They could also be required to attend on those who were to be executed, and the notes given to Guilford in 1917, detailed in Chapter 2, set out the following duties for a chaplain:

Ascertain the prisoner's denomination and arrange for services of a Chaplain. The Chaplain will attend the promulgation of the sentence to the prisoner and will inform the latter when it will be carried out. He may remain with the prisoner up to the time the latter is prepared for execution (ie when the APM enters the place of confinement and demands the prisoner from the guard) and will not be allowed further intercourse with him after that time. He may attend the execution and he will afterwards read the burial service. It is undesirable that he should wear vestments.

In civilian prisons, ministering to the condemned was seen as a highly specialised role, left to prison chaplains or to exemplary pastors, but this was not explicitly the case where military executions were concerned, although it does appear to have been devolved to those who were more experienced. Snape observes that because of the numbers of army chaplains on the Western Front and the small number of men executed, the number of chaplains who were called upon to attend executions was, in turn, quite small. Many death sentences – Snape says 89 per cent – were commuted at the eleventh hour, meaning that more clergy would have experienced preparing a man for death whose sentence was subsequently commuted, than were involved in an actual execution.

If a civilian had been condemned to death, the legal process involved led to many weeks passing between sentence and execution, giving a prison chaplain a considerable amount of time to spend with the condemned and allowing them to repent and be reconciled with God. This was not the case in the military where there were usually only days or just hours between promulgation of sentence and the execution of that sentence, meaning that the focus was on ensuring that the condemned 'died a good death' (Snape). Some chaplains were prepared to offer practical help in addition to spiritual assistance to the condemned, such as the provision of alcohol, pills to help them sleep better, letter writing, or accepting personal items to be passed on to family and loved ones.

Although the army required a chaplain to be present, it was still the condemned man's choice as to whether or not to avail themselves of his services. In 1915, Captain T.H. Westmacott had been appointed the APM of the 1st Indian Cavalry Division, and his duties included being present at executions. On one occasion he attended the execution of a soldier from the 29th Lancers and noted (Brown, 2001): 'Gibbon, the Divisional Chaplain, was a great nuisance, as he obtained leave from the Divisional Commander to visit Yadram during the night. As Yadram was a Jat and not a Christian we all considered it a great piece of impertinence on Gibbon's part.'

† † †

The role of the condemned man's church and the army chaplain is not as simple as it may first be thought. For the condemned man who has just found out that he is to be executed in a matter of hours, the army chaplain may have been the friendly face that they craved – however, they were far from being a friend at that time. The army chaplains were, in fact, part of the military establishment and as Snape states: 'No case has come to light during the course of this research of any chaplain condemning a capital sentence passed by a court martial.' Brigadier F.P. Crozier (1930) noted that what seemed to exercise the clergy more than anything was the condemned man's access to alcohol prior to their execution.

The Society for the Abolition of Capital Punishment carried out a survey of ecclesiastical opinion in 1900 and found that all those who took part supported the state's right to carry out executions, relying on Genesis 9.6 as justification: 'Whoever sheds the blood of man, by man shall his blood be shed.' Where British Army executions in the period August 1914 to March 1920 are concerned, only fifteen British soldiers were executed for murder, while the remainder were executed for offences that did not exist in civilian law (Snape), therefore making the clergy's support for military executions questionable. The vast majority of British soldiers executed had not committed an offence that had its equivalent in civilian law or could be categorised as a sin. As Brigadier Crozier (1937), a supporter of military executions, pointed out in connection with the execution of Private James Crozier of the 9th Royal Irish Rifles on 27 February 1916: having committed no specific sin, 'Why the culprit had to make his peace with God when the only trouble he had at the time was with the commander-in-chief of the British Armies in France, I do not know.'

It can be said, therefore, that army chaplains supported the death penalty – thereby producing a tension between their role ministering to the condemned and their place in the establishment, which would almost certainly have been too subtle for the condemned man to understand. In addition, as Snape says, the army chaplains, who were both educated and commissioned, would have had little in common with the majority of those men sentenced to death.

Even without the First World War, the world of 1914 to 1918 was vastly different from that of today, so that must temper any criticism of their conduct and views. However, if anyone at the time could voice opposition to what was happening, then it would have been the churches, and the army chaplains would have been best placed to do so, but they supported the death penalty and therefore never saw the need to do so.

† † †

Reverend Julian Bickersteth of the 56th Division was in attendance at the execution of Private Walter Yeoman of the 1/12th Royal Fusiliers on 3 July 1917. Yeoman was a soldier who had been sentenced for the offence of desertion. Bickersteth had got to know Yeoman over a number of months, and asked the senior chaplain, who had decided to attend the execution himself, if he could go instead. His diary entry, contained in a long letter he wrote on 5 July 1917, provides a very moving account of the build-up to Private Yeoman's execution.

Bickersteth (1996) spent the twelve hours between the promulgation of the sentence and the execution itself with Yeoman in a room that he described as only 'nine feet by ten feet' and with two guards in attendance, so there was no opportunity for any privacy. Bickersteth, in a very detailed letter to his brother, recalled saying to Yeoman, 'I am going to stay with you and do anything I can for you. If you'd like to talk, we will, but if you'd rather not, we'll sit quiet.'

Yeoman was initially unresponsive to Bickersteth's ministry but eventually said that he wanted to sing hymns, which they did for three hours, finishing eventually, if somewhat ironically in the circumstances, with 'God Save the King'. Bickersteth realised that the words to the hymns had themselves meant nothing to the condemned man, but that he perhaps made himself feel better by convincing himself that they were, in fact, a form of prayer and that therefore they had, indeed, prayed together. Bickersteth stayed with Yeoman all night while one sentry played patience and the other read a book. Earlier he had used a sentry's knife to put jam on Private Yeoman's bread as the condemned man was not permitted to use a knife himself.

At dawn, with preparations under way for the execution, Bickersteth was given rum for the condemned man by the APM. In fact, Yeoman refused it but enjoyed his breakfast of bread, butter, ham and tea. When Yeoman was tied securely to the stake, Bickersteth whispered in his ear, 'Safe in the arms of Jesus', and Yeoman replied, 'Safe in the arms of Jesus'.

Bickersteth was also in attendance at the execution of Private Henry Williams of the 1/9th Royal Fusiliers on 28 December 1917 for the offence of desertion. His diary shows that he found the experience physically and mentally trying and wrote of the 'simple heroism of this mere lad of nineteen, who has been out here at the front since 1914'.

He spent the night with the condemned man, hearing what Bickersteth said was Williams' first and last confession. He said that Williams:

gave me all his little treasures to give to this friend or that. He wrote a letter to his sweetheart and sent her his letter with all its photographs and trinkets, a lucky farthing which she had given him for a keepsake, his last 'leave' ticket, and other small things.

In his diaries (1996), he recalled the condemned man's final moments:

As they bound him, I held his arm tight to reassure him – words are useless at such a moment – and then he turned his blindfolded face up to mine and said in a voice that wrung my heart, 'Kiss me, Sir, kiss me,' and with my kiss on his lips and, 'God has you in his keeping,' whispered in his ear, he passed on into the Great unseen. God accept him; receive him.

Bickersteth (Holmes, 2005) had sufficient awareness to realise that it was not just the condemned man who needed comforting and, following an execution, he spent time talking to those in the firing squad and giving them cigarettes, but he does not reveal any views in his letters or diary entries that show that he opposed the death penalty. It must be assumed, therefore, that despite everything he supported it.

An example of a last letter home, in this case from Private Albert Troughton, can be found in Appendix 4.

† † †

Another army chaplain, Martin Andrews, was present for the execution of Private Alfred Ansted of the 4th Royal Fusiliers. Ansted was executed on 15 November 1916 having been found guilty of desertion. In addition to his official duties, Andrews brought Ansted two pills to 'put in his tea' and 'which would make him sleep better'.

The Reverend Harry Blackburne (1932) was required to officiate at the double execution of Lance-Corporal William Price and Private Richard Morgan, 2nd Welsh Regiment. Both men had been found guilty of murder and were executed on 15 February 1915. On the night before the execution, he read them the parable of the prodigal son and then prayed with them; in a letter to his wife, he said, 'now I must go and be with them to the end. Thank God, it is all over' (Putkowski and Dunning, 2012).

Captain T. Guy Rogers, MC, who was chaplain to the 2nd Guards Brigade, was ordered to attend the execution of Private H.T.W. Phillips, 1st Coldstream Guards, which took place on 30 May 1916, for the offence of desertion. In his letters, kept at the Imperial War Museum, Rogers wrote:

It has just fallen to my lot to prepare a deserter for his death – that meant breaking the news to him, helping him with his last letters, passing the night with him on the straw in his cell, and trying to prepare his soul for meeting God: the execution and burying him immediately ... Monday night I was with him, Tuesday morning at 3.30 he was shot. He lay beside me for hours with his hand in mine. Poor fellow, it was a bad case, but he met his end bravely, and drank all I could teach him about God, his father, Jesus his Saviour, the reality of forgiveness of sins. I feel shaken by it all, but my nerves, thank God, have not troubled me.

Although this letter demonstrates some sympathy for the plight of Private Phillips, there is again no indication that Rogers actually opposed the sentence, whereas there is more than a suggestion of feeling sorry for himself and of wanting the reader of the letter to share those feelings.

† † †

However, although not in the British Army, one chaplain, Canon F.G. Scott, senior chaplain to the 1st Canadian Division, did try to stop an execution going ahead, and his recollections are valid in the context of this book. The condemned man is not named by Scott but Putkowski and Sykes (1998) have identified him as Company Quartermaster Sergeant William Alexander of the 10th Canadian Expeditionary Force (Alberta Regiment). Alexander's offence was desertion; however, despite Scott lobbying senior officers on two occasions, the execution went ahead on 18 October 1917.

Alexander was in a cell under guard when Scott arrived, sitting at a table with a bottle of brandy and writing materials. In the ensuing conversation, Alexander revealed that he had never been baptised and in the time that was left this was something that he wished to rectify, so Scott performed what must have been one of the bleakest baptisms he ever carried out. Scott was impressed by the man and said, 'I kept wondering if I could not even then, at that late hour, do something to avert the carrying out of the sentence.'

Keeping his feelings to himself and certainly not giving hope to Alexander, as that would have been cruel, in the early hours of the morning Scott walked to army headquarters to ask the army commander, a general, to commute Alexander's sentence. The general explained to Scott that, as the due process had been followed and the sentence had been confirmed by the British commander-in-chief, Sir Douglas Haig, the decision would stand unless new evidence could be presented. The general suggested that mental weakness or insanity might cause a stay of execution and a new trial, which gave Scott some hope.

When he returned to Alexander's cell, Scott was able to steer the conversation and found that there was a history of mental weakness on both sides of the condemned man's family. Armed with this information, he returned to army headquarters and again saw the general, who said that Scott needed to see the divisional commander. With time running out, Scott got to see the divisional commander and spoke for Alexander, only to be told that as the court martial had carefully considered the case, then the final decision would stand. The divisional commander added that to delay the execution, even for twenty-four hours, only for it to then go ahead, was adding an avoidable level of mental torture for the condemned. Scott could only agree.

By the time Scott returned, Alexander had somehow found out what had been attempted. Scott told him, 'Everyone is longing just as much as I am to save you, but the matter has been gone into so carefully and has gone so far, and so much depends upon every man doing his duty to the uttermost, that the sentence must be carried out.'

Scott describes the execution in some detail – one of the most notable points of which was that Alexander, despite his pleas to have his eyes left uncovered, had his head covered by a gas mask which was put on back to front. As Scott states, the condemned man wearing a blindfold would have been for the benefit of the firing squad because the effect of seeing the victim's face had been known to lead to the men firing wide.

The medical officer and Scott had retired beyond a hedge out of sight of the execution, but no amount of putting their hands over their ears could keep out the sound of the volley. Scott then spoke to the members of the firing squad, telling them 'how deeply all ranks felt the occasion, and that nothing but the dire necessity of guarding the lives of the men in the front line from the panic and rout that might result through the failure of one individual, compelled the taking of such measures of punishment'.

Despite everything, though, even when writing his memoirs, Scott still could not bring himself to oppose the legitimacy of the death sentence.

† † †

Edward Montmorency ('Monty') Guilford, MC was a Church of England chaplain to the Oxfordshire and Buckinghamshire Light Infantry when he was told to attend an execution, at which time he received a copy of the notes referred to in Chapter 2 (Fiennes, 2012). The condemned man was Private Joseph Bateman of the 2nd South Staffordshire Regiment, who was executed for desertion on 3 December 1917.

It was the chaplain's job to identify a grave site for Bateman's body and to ensure that it was dug and ready. Guilford was to remain with Bateman for the twelve hours between the promulgation and the carrying out of the sentence, during which time he wrote down a letter that the condemned dictated to him. Then finally he read the burial service over the hastily filled-in grave.

Fiennes feels that Guilford at the time supported the use of the death penalty in wartime but that it was an experience that haunted him for the rest of his life.

The Reverend R.H.J. Steuart was a Roman Catholic chaplain to a battalion of the Highland Light Infantry in the 15th Scottish Division (1916–18) and, from January 1918, in the 35th (Bantam) Division. He was detailed to attend the execution of Corporal C. Lewis, 12th Highland Light Infantry, which was carried out on 11 March 1916, and also that of Private Hector Dalande of the 8th Seaforth Highlanders. Dalande had been found guilty of desertion and was executed on 9 March 1918.

Steuart describes finding a distraught Dalande in his cell and goes on to relate details of the execution. A blindfold was placed over his eyes, his hands were tied behind his back, and a small piece of lint was pinned over his heart by the medical officer. As for Steuart: 'I kept my hand upon his arm as we walked, and I can vouch for it that he never faltered nor trembled.'

Despite recalling the distinct 'thrill of repugnance' where attending an execution was concerned, Steuart did not argue against the use of the death penalty.

Father Benedict Williamson, a Roman Catholic padre in the 47th Division, attended the execution of Private Patrick Murphy of the 47th Battalion, Machine Gun Corps, which took place on 12 September 1918, for the offence of desertion. Williamson (2005) wrote of the distress felt by all those involved because 'there is an immense difference between seeing a number of men slain in battle and seeing one shot with all the cold deliberation that follows in such a case as this.'

Williamson had spent some time praying with Murphy and hearing his confession. This was another occasion when the chaplain concerned was to be impressed by the fortitude of the condemned man, though seemingly without opposing the sentence imposed, as Williamson made the following observations: 'I spent some time encouraging him for the fiery ordeal he would soon pass through. The scene almost carried one back to the days of the martyrs, the boy was so wonderfully calm and resigned.'

Williamson walked with Murphy to the place of execution and in the final moments prayed with him. Murphy's final words were, 'Goodbye Father.'

The Church has always seemed able to turn a human tragedy into something positive, and Williamson felt able to attribute Murphy's bravery at the end to the Catholic religion, saying, 'I have never in the course of my experience assisted at a death more consoling or one in which I felt more absolute assurance of the state of the soul going forth to God.'

Murphy had been barely 20 when he had enlisted in August 1914 and yet there is no discernible recognition, or concern, in Williamson's words about a young life being terminated under such circumstances.

† † †

As previously mentioned, the role of an army chaplain was, above all, to raise the men's morale and to foster discipline, so it could be argued that military executions represented something of a failure on the part of the Church. However, this does not appear to have been a problem, as the Church in the early years of the twentieth century supported the death penalty in both the military and the civilian worlds.

The churches based this support on Genesis (9.6), which states, 'Whoever sheds the blood of man, by man shall his blood be shed.' But where military executions were concerned, this surely could only be an argument in favour of the fifteen executions for murder. The vast majority of executions were for offences that had no civilian equivalent and, furthermore, were not sins against God.

Faced with an execution, the role of the army chaplain was to help the condemned man prepare to ensure that he 'died a good death', whatever that might mean. Given that the amount of time between the promulgation of sentence and the carrying out of the sentence was sometimes just a matter of hours, the army chaplain did not have long to achieve this objective; however, many did help the men concerned, providing practical help in addition to the religious side of their role.

There is, though, a paradox here, as the army chaplain was the condemned man's only friendly face, and yet the man behind that face would have wholeheartedly supported the death penalty, and was someone who was a commissioned officer, and therefore part of the military establishment, which meant that they were never truly on the side of the condemned man. In addition, there is no recorded evidence that an army chaplain ever condemned the death penalty, not even in those moments following an execution when emotions would have been heightened.

In terms of the notes passed to Guilford, the army chaplains did fulfil that role and, from the evidence gathered above, they can be seen, in many cases, to have gone further in support of the condemned man. The Church, and its army chaplains, would have been in a position to argue against the death penalty and exert pressure for change, but it never did because at that time it supported the death penalty, although perhaps for wrong-headed reasons.

5

THE MEDICAL OFFICER

The army medical officer's primary role in conflict was to save the lives of those wounded on the battlefield and to tend to those who were sick. As the notes given to Guilford in 1917 show, however, there could be occasions when the focus was on facilitating the end of life at an execution. Private Walter Williams (Williams, 2013) commented in his memoirs that, with medical staff being overworked because they were dealing with the inevitable battle casualties, he found it remarkable that doctors could be found 'who were willing to take part in this ghastly charade'.

Despite the growing awareness of shell shock, one medical officer said, 'I went to the trial determined to give him no help of any sort, for I detest his type … I really hoped he would be shot' (Holden, 1998). This represented a view that if you gave what many, including this medical officer, saw as plain and simple cowardice an acceptable name – such as shell shock – then it would somehow validate the actions of those men who were unwilling to fight and thereby undermine army discipline in the field: a form of absenteeism that would be recognisable today in the civilian sector of society. There were, therefore, medical officers who would willingly have been present at executions because they believed in the death sentence, in line with their military training, the military culture and the standards of the time.

The notes issued to Guilford set out the following aspects associated with the role of a medical officer at an execution:

Arrange with the Assistant Director Medical Services for the presence of a Medical Officer at the execution.

The Medical Officer will provide a three cornered bandage for blindfolding and a small paper disc for fixing over the heart. He will adjust these when requested by the APM.

He will also arrange for a stretcher in case the prisoner is unable to walk.

The Medical Officer will go forward and examine the body. If he considers that life is not extinct he will summon the Officer i/c of the firing party, who will complete the sentence with his revolver.

The Medical Officer will certify death and sign the death certificate which he will hand to the APM.

✝ ✝ ✝

Captain M.S. Esler was the medical officer with the 8th Division, 2nd Middlesex Regiment (Brown, 2001), when he was ordered to be present at the execution of Private Frank O'Neill, 1st Sherwood Foresters, on 16 May 1918. On giving him his orders to attend, Esler was told by his commanding officer that: 'He knew I should hate it as much as he did.'

Esler had to pin a red piece of paper over O'Neill's heart after the condemned man had turned down his offer of half a pint of brandy, on the basis that he had never drunk spirits before and was not about to start then. Esler said that he had seen many men shot, 'but never one of our own men by our men, and it made me feel very sick, I who thought that I had grown hardened to death'.

Captain L. Gameson spent the war attached to various units in the 15th Division, but by August 1919 he was with the 5th Army Headquarters in Lille when he was ordered to attend the executions of Privates Willie Harris and Abraham Davids of the 1st Cape Coloured Labour Regiment. The two men had been found guilty of murder and were to be executed on 26 August 1919.

Gameson had been chosen by the assistant director of medical services because the APM had complained 'that the last MO supplied to him fainted during the proceedings. He wants me to provide one who won't. I am therefore detailing you.'

The APM told Gameson when they met that he was to give the two men a heavy dose of morphia but not enough to render them incapable of walking. Gameson had misgivings about what he was being told to do because 'people vary in their reactions to that drug, both as to the reaction and the time necessary to produce it. I gave each victim a large enough dose to ensure the required result.'

When the two men were calm enough for him he proceeded to the next step which was to pin two envelopes, the targets, to the men's shirts:

Of the many distasteful duties which have inevitably come my way, what followed stayed in my mind as the worst. The men were clothed in thin shirts, tight, close fitting intentionally. I had to percuss out cardiac areas, identify apex-beats, pin envelopes to the shirts. To do this while meeting these men's eyes looking into my eyes was humiliating and shocking. I blindfolded them.

Gameson had been told that he had to stand as near to the two staked men as possible so as to reach them as soon as was possible following the deadly volley and to check for life.

There could also be risks for those in attendance: it was on this occasion that Gameson himself was nearly shot when a sergeant was loading the rifles and one accidentally went off, resulting in the bullet narrowly missing his head.

Gameson could have testified that lightning does indeed strike twice when he was called upon to attend the execution of Private F. Boos, also known as Alberts, of the 1st Cape Coloured Regiment on 15 October 1919, also for the offence of murder. On this occasion the firing squad failed to kill Boos outright and Gameson, examining him, told the sergeant in charge that Boos still lived. The sergeant, almost certainly through a mixture of anxiety and haste, shot Boos through the head before checking that Gameson had moved safely away. The bullet passed straight through Boos' head and fortunately just over Gameson's head. Gameson, lucky to be alive, was able to describe the execution as 'a messy and disturbing business'.

Guilford's notes were issued in respect of Private Joseph Bateman, and the record of the field general court martial (file WO71/621 held at The National Archives) shows that Private Bateman's death was certified by Captain T. Bourne-Price (RAMC) with the comment that 'death was instantaneous'. On another occasion (WO71/556) the medical officer present when Private William Bowerman, of the 1st East Surrey Regiment, was executed for desertion on 24 March 1917, recorded that his 'death was not instantaneous'.

† † †

The evidence available shows that some army medical officers did not accept shell shock as a battlefield condition and took the view that its recognition would have given cowardice an acceptable name. This, in turn, would have coloured their approach to courts martial and the death sentence. In terms of the notes given to Guilford, the army medical officers appear to have fulfilled the role set down for them.

What also is starting to emerge is the influence of the APM on the conduct of military executions – for example, insisting on an army medical officer who would not faint, seeking the adjustment of the target disc, and requesting that drugs, such as morphia, be administered to the condemned man – and this is something that will now be discussed further.

6

THE MILITARY POLICE AND THE ASSISTANT PROVOST MARSHAL

In the same way that the death penalty in the military can be traced back to the fourteenth century, so too can the post of the provost marshal, who was responsible, according to the Royal Military Police Museum (RMP Museum), 'for maintaining the peace "12 miles about the Prince's person", and dealt summarily with all offenders, military and civilian alike'. The provost marshal held the rank of colonel until 1915 when the rank changed to that of brigadier.

The first mention of the word 'police' in connection with the military was in a War Office circular published on 13 June 1855 which created the Corps of Military Mounted Police. Certain cavalry regiments were told to provide non-commissioned officers (NCOs) of 'five or ten years' service, sober habits, intelligent, active and capable of exercising a sound discretion', to be based at Aldershot 'for the preservation of Good Order in the camp at Aldershot, and for the protection of the inhabitants of the neighbourhood'. (RMP Museum)

The Corps of Military Foot Police was created on 1 August 1882 for service in Egypt and consisted entirely of men who, in civilian life, had served with the Metropolitan Police. The corps' existence was made permanent on 2 July 1885 with an establishment of: '1 sergeant-major; 13 sergeants; 17 corporals;

and 59 privates. The end of the century saw the Military Police with a strength of just over 300.' (RMP Museum) The two corps would eventually be combined in 1926.

At the outbreak of the First World War, the total military police strength was 508, which quickly increased to 761 with the recall of reservists, many of whom had been policemen in civilian life. By 1918 the corps had over 25,000 men of all ranks (RMP Museum).

It was the crimson red covering of their peaked caps and the black cloth armband with the letters 'MP' that distinguished the military police from the other troops on the Western Front. As the war progressed they were issued with steel helmets with 'MP' painted on the front. If the military police were to help maintain discipline then there was the expectation, in turn, that they would be well turned out at all times.

In 1914, the military police operated what were referred to as 'stragglers' posts', used, for example, during the retreat from Mons, which would return soldiers to their units if they had become separated. In addition, these posts might also detect and arrest those thought to have deserted. On occasions, though, the military police would simply shoot those running away, and it is not known how many were 'executed' in this way, but it could be in excess of the number officially executed. One military policeman, when questioned about what he had done during the war, replied with conviction, 'Damn it, I was standing behind the lines shooting them that were running away'.

Brigadier Crozier (1937), who has received several mentions in this book, claimed to have shot at least one of his own men and ordered his men to machine-gun Portuguese troops who were running away. He justified this by saying, 'Men will not, as a rule, risk their lives unnecessarily unless they know that they will be shot down by their own officers if they fail to do so or if they waver.'

✝ ✝ ✝

Military police matters came under the office of the adjutant-general and on his behalf, the provost marshal supervised military police duties of the army in the field. The adjutant-general and the provost marshal were represented at every level of the military hierarchy, as defined by Banning (1923):

A general officer, commanding a body of troops abroad, may appoint a Provost-Marshal, who will always be a commissioned officer; his assistants may be officers or non-commissioned officers. His duties are to arrest offenders and he may carry into execution any punishments inflicted by sentence of court martial, but he no longer has any power to inflict punishment on his own authority.

Therefore, each of the British Army divisions on the Western Front had one assistant provost marshal (APM) with the rank of captain or major, together with a number of non-commissioned officers; the APM received his orders from the divisional assistant adjutant-general, and was responsible for organising the police under his command.

† † †

The notes given to Guilford make the following references to the APM and the military police:

Settle day and hour of execution. APM to inform Divisional Headquarters.

Prisoner to be handed over to a guard of his own unit. The NCO in command of the guard to be of full rank and to be specially selected. He will receive instructions from the APM.

He may remain with the prisoner up to the time the latter is prepared for execution (ie when the APM enters the place of confinement and demands the prisoner from the guard).

<u>Military police</u>
Military Police will be employed to prevent traffic from passing by the place of execution for half an hour before the hour fixed for execution and until all traces of its having taken place have been removed.

The Officer will be present at the promulgation of the sentence to the prisoner and will on that occasion receive from the APM any instructions as necessary.

The APM is responsible for all arrangements and for seeing the sentence carried out.

The APM will collect pay book and identification disc and make them over to the NCO in charge of the guard for delivery at the unit's Orderly Room.

The Medical Officer will provide a three cornered bandage for blindfolding and a small paper disc for fixing over the heart. He will adjust these when requested by the APM.

The firing party will be marched into position by the APM whilst the prisoner is being tied to the post. The APM will so time this that the firing party will be ready for action simultaneously with the completion of the tying up.

The firing party will march in two ranks, halt on the rifles, turn to the right or left, pick up the rifles and come to a ready position, front rank kneeling, rear rank standing. They will press forward safety catch and come to the 'present' on a signal from the APM. The Officer, when he sees all the men are steady, will give the word 'fire'. This is to be the only word of command given after the prisoner leaves the place of confinement.

✝ ✝ ✝

The notes issued to Guilford make clear that the medical officer's first action would be to 'provide a three cornered bandage for blindfolding', but this, contrary to public perception, was not done as an act of humanity towards the condemned but rather to save the firing squad from having to look into the man's eyes, because as discussed earlier, that was the weak link in the execution chain.

Sergeant Len Cavinder of the 1/4th East Yorkshire Regiment was present at the execution of Private Charles McColl; Cavinder and another man were detailed to escort McColl from a military prison at Brandhoek to a prison at Ypres (Corns and Hughes-Wilson), the prisoner at that stage being unaware of his fate. It fell to Sergeant Cavinder and his fellow guard to bury Private McColl's body at the conclusion of the execution.

Canon Scott (1922) recalled seeing a man (this was in all probability Private Charles McColl of the 1/4th East Yorkshire Regiment who was executed for desertion on 28 December 1917) prepared for his execution by having a gas mask placed over his head, but back to front so that the eye pieces were at the back. The gas masks were made of flannel and the wearer breathed in through the flannel itself and out through the attached tube – they were unpopular to wear even when under a gas attack. With the helmet on back to front, this would only have added to the horror of the moment for both the condemned man and the firing party.

Who would have decided that this was appropriate, stripping the condemned man of the last vestiges of dignity in his final moments? Canon Scott recalled that it had been the APM who had officiated at this execution and therefore the likelihood is that this would have been his decision because it is unlikely to have been an order passed down the chain of command. If so, it demonstrates that a degree of inhumanity, if not sadism, was present during the last moments of some of those shot.

The notes given to Guilford reveal the central role played by the APM, and the holders of this post were not generally well liked. It is likely that an APM would have been present at more executions than other officers in a division and so would have been looked to for their experience; therefore they wielded considerable influence as to how matters were conducted.

Private James Adamson of the 7th Camerons was executed on 23 November 1917 having been found guilty of coward-ice. His execution was recalled in the memoirs of Trooper G.S. Chaplin who was a member of the Mounted Military Police (Putkowski and Sykes, 1996). On the morning of the execution, Chaplin had been sent up the road to stop any traffic, maintaining the army's instructions to avoid bystand-ers, although it could be argued that allowing those passing to see what was happening would have reinforced the deterrent aspect of the sentence. His memoirs include his assessment of the APM as being 'beneath contempt'.

††††

Étaples was a sprawling base camp in Northern France some 5km from the English Channel. It was an unpopular place with those who found themselves there for training or rehabilita-tion due to the petty and repressive regime they experienced, imposed by the instructors and the large number of military police. It was here, over six days in September 1917, that a size-able number of men from the British Army mutinied, thereby threatening the autumn offensive at Passchendaele, much to the consternation of Sir Douglas Haig, the commander-in-chief.

The catalyst for the mutiny was the killing of 'an inof-fensive man by an excited military policeman' (Brown, 2001). On 9 September 1917, Corporal Gordon Wood, of the 4th Gordon Highlanders, had decided to leave his compound and set off for a visit to the cinema, but on the way he stopped to talk to a girl from the WAAC. Unfortunately for Wood, a military policemen, Private Harry Reeve, came by and saw him lounging around with his tunic buttons undone, talking to the young WAAC. Private Reeve was both a boxing cham-pion and had a reputation as a bully (Allison and Fairley, 1986), and he ordered Corporal Wood to move on, pointing out that he was improperly dressed. The two men argued, whereupon Private Reeve shot and fatally wounded Corporal Wood.

When news of what had occurred spread around the camp, the soldiers erupted in fury and the military police, already the focus of many grievances, had to take flight. They were hunted down and many were badly beaten or killed in the process, despite having been given temporary shelter in local homes. It was an event that led to the brief breakdown of all discipline in the camp.

Allison and Fairley's book, entitled *The Monocled Mutineer*, is a very interesting read, as it describes the story of this not inconsiderable mutiny in detail; there is no need to retell the story here, except to highlight the way that the news of the event and its aftermath were handled.

According to Allison and Fairley, the official records do not mention the scale of the problem, and Sir Douglas Haig went to great lengths to avoid his nemesis David Lloyd George, the prime minister, finding out the true picture, as he feared giving his adversary an excuse to replace him. This was a demonstration of the commander-in-chief living by his mantra that 'truth could be abandoned in the cause of the war effort'. This lack of transparency will be further discussed in the later chapters on abolition and pardons.

Lady Angela Forbes, who was no friend of the commander-in-chief, was much loved by the soldiers, having set up a tea-and-bun hut in the middle of the camp. She was an independent witness of what had gone on at Étaples and therefore Sir Douglas Haig ordered that she was to be sent back to Britain. Again, the details of this episode are well set out in *The Monocled Mutineer* and so do not need to be covered here other than to repeat Lady Angela's concern 'at the cruel conduct of the military policemen', which she maintained was a reflection of their commander, Assistant Provost Marshal Strachan.

There is also a lack of transparency over what happened to those soldiers who were deemed to be the ringleaders of the mutiny once it had ended. Allison and Fairley state that ten men were eventually shot, and yet the official records only admit to three men in the whole war having been executed for mutiny. To confuse matters further, whilst Corns and Hughes-Wilson list four men who were executed for mutiny, two were killed on 29 October 1916 – which predates the mutiny – with the remaining two being executed in October 1917.

It is possible, therefore, that Labourer Ahmed Mahmoud Mohamed of the Egypt Labour Corps, who was executed on 20 October, and Private Thomas Davis of the 1st Royal Munsters Regiment, who was executed on 4 October, were involved in the events at Étaples.

† † †

Military policemen, also known as 'redcaps' because of the red band around their caps, could be just as affected by an execution as the next man (Moore, 1999), as shown when one of their number entered a small café in a distressed state and desperate for company. Having found a friendly ear, or at least someone who was prepared to share a table with a military policeman, he told of his experiences the previous night guarding a man who had then been shot that morning. It seemed that just before the condemned man was taken away, he had given his cigarettes and matches, together with a few coins, to the military policeman, saying, 'I shan't need these. You'd better have them.'

From the evidence available, the picture that begins to emerge is one where the APM was a central figure regarding the organisation of the executions. The regimental officers, in the absence of regulations governing the conduct of executions, were only too happy to defer to a figure who would have more experience than them in such matters, and this gave rise to the variations that occurred.

The mutiny at Étaples resulted from the actions of a military policeman, and Private Reeve appears to be the public face of a regime typified by calculated cruelty on the part of the base's instructors and military police, and indifference to the treatment of the men by the officers who were charged with their care.

Another aspect arising from the mutiny at Étaples is the way that the military hierarchy sought to cover up the extent of events there and seem to have manipulated the facts in accordance with Sir Douglas Haig's mantra, mentioned earlier. This will be explored further in a later chapter.

7

ABOLITION OF THE DEATH PENALTY IN THE BRITISH ARMY

The campaign to abolish the death penalty started in 1915 and finally achieved its objective by 1930, having been fought out in the Houses of Parliament and in and around Westminster. The case for abolition was based, by and large, on moral, ethical and logical grounds, but those involved did not seek pardons for those executed. The campaign for pardons got underway in 1989 and ended successfully in 2006, involving and engaging the public much more, although its final battle was again to be fought in the Houses of Parliament and Westminster.

†††

still done in prisons in the 1950s

The final public execution in England took place on 26 May 1868 when Michael Barrett was hung at Newgate for the Fenian bombing at Clerkenwell, yet 'public' executions were still taking place on the Western Front throughout the First World War because, on occasions, at the apparent whim of their commanding officer, regiments and battalions were paraded to witness the event.

Private Thomas Highgate, as discussed earlier, was executed on 8 September 1914, having been sentenced to death for desertion. Private Highgate served in the 1st Battalion

The execution post at Poperinghe, against which men such as Private James Michael were shot. Private Michael of the 10th Battalion Cameronians, Scottish Rifles, was shot at dawn for desertion on 24 August 1917. He had gone absent during the opening of the Third Battle of Ypres in July. Private Herbert Morris was recruited in the West Indies during the winter of 1916/17. As he was black, he was never intended to be a combatant. He went absent, he said, because he could not cope with the sound of the guns. At 17 he was one of the youngest to be shot – though not the only one underage. (Courtesy of Paul Kendall)

of the Royal West Kents, which was one of the first elements of the British Expeditionary Force to land in France on 15 August 1914 and took part in the fighting at Mons. General Sir Horace Smith-Dorrien decided when confirming the sentence to make a very public example of Highgate and ordered that he 'should be killed as publicly as possible' (Hastings, 2013). As a result, he was executed in front of two companies of his comrades. Smith-Dorrien later justified this by claiming that, as a result, there were no further charges of desertion brought in his division and, therefore, deterrence worked.

After the war, an MP recalled being told by a general that he had 'paraded the whole division in order to see the sentence carried out' (Moore, 1999). On 22 May 1916, Private William Burrell of the 2nd Sussex Regiment was shot for desertion. Private Burrell was executed in front of his comrades, who were ordered to face away from the place of execution and told that anyone who turned around would be placed on a charge. Such was the strain on the men present that one man fainted as the shots rang out.

As brutal as such public executions may seem today, the military hierarchy justified them on the grounds that there would have been no purpose in executing a soldier except in front of his comrades, where it would serve as a deterrent to others. But as Private Walter Williams of the Machine Gun Corps/Northumberland Fusiliers (Williams, 2013) shows in his memoirs, this was not always the effect achieved. Williams wrote about the emotional aftermath of having to witness, along with many other soldiers, the execution of a man from his own regiment. When the men had fallen out after the execution, a number expressed their anger at what they had just seen by swearing, cursing the injustice, and breaking whatever was to hand, while others prayed. The men were united in the view that the execution was not the deterrent the army had hoped for and that their officers had lost all respect. This was surely not the effect the officers concerned would have hoped for or expected?

It was also likely that the First World War, perhaps more than any conflict that had gone before, piled horror upon horror on those involved, and therefore the effect of witnessing an execution became diluted as the war progressed.

The deterrent aspect of the executions was further undermined by the fact that a number of men who had been shot for desertion were serial offenders – they had been tried and sentenced to death, but the sentence had been commuted two, three and sometimes four times before their luck finally ran out. By way of an example, Private Frederick Broadrick of the Royal Warwickshire Regiment was serving with its 11th Battalion while already subject to a suspended death sentence, when he deserted again rather than parade for a working party to which he had been detailed; he was executed on 1 August 1917. Private Samuel Cunningham, also from the Royal Warwickshire Regiment, who had enlisted in January 1914, was sentenced to twenty-eight days' detention for desertion on 21 January 1916. Undeterred, he deserted again; after his eventual capture, at a court martial held on 29 April 1917, he was found guilty and sentenced to death. He was executed on 19 May 1917.

The Reverend Julian Bickersteth wrote in his diary on 5 July 1917 about Private Walter Yeoman, who had deserted a further four times since his initial act of desertion. The man had had his death sentence commuted and then suspended to give him another chance, but he had deserted again.

The evidence, therefore, as limited as it might appear, points to this being an aspect of military executions where there was no consistency, as not all executions were carried out with the condemned man's battalion or regiment present, which undermined the only logical reason for executions, namely deterrence. As will be discussed later, some soldiers simply did not believe that they took place at all.

† † †

From 1915 onwards, uncomfortable questions about the army's use of the death penalty began to be asked in Parliament. In

1915, Under Secretary of State for War Harold Tennant, in answer to a direct question, confirmed that executions had taken place, but in July of that year he refused to confirm the number of death sentences passed, on the grounds that it would not be in the public interest. Over the subsequent years the questions were to continue.

In 1919, the army showed that it was aware of the public mood and the likely consequences for its ability to retain the death penalty, as evidenced in the following extract from Public Record Office file 'WO32/5479 Suspension of the Death Penalty: 1918–19':

> 'Even during the continuance of hostilities there was very strong feeling both in the country and in the House of Commons against the infliction of the death penalty for military offences. Now that hostilities have ceased it can confidently be stated that the effect on this country of a death penalty might lead to an agitation which might be difficult to control and in all probability would jeopardise the prospects of maintaining the death penalty for military offences in time of peace when the Annual Army (Act) comes before the Houses of Parliament.' 2nd March 1919 D.P.S. [Director of Personal Services] Brigadier General Sir Wyndham Childs (Department of the Adjutant General)

The Darling Committee Report in 1919 effectively gave a clean bill of health to the court martial system of the time despite three committee members refusing to sign the report. These individuals then submitted their own report, which differed from the majority report in many areas. Specifically, they complained that investigations into miscarriages of justice had been blocked and, although such instances were evident, they had been unable to investigate further. They also concluded that there had been too many courts martial during the war, court martial panel members should have legal training, the confirmation-of-sentence process should be removed, and that a right of appeal should be introduced.

In 1920, a War Office committee of inquiry was set up, under the chairmanship of Lord Southborough, to look into the different types of hysteria and traumatic neurosis and, not surprisingly, this was referred to as the Shell Shock Committee, which reported back two years later. As a result of its deliberations, it brought together knowledge of these conditions and treatment methods and Corns and Hughes-Wilson provided a detailed examination of the work of this committee.

One of the witnesses called was Captain James Churchill Dunn, DSO, MC and Bar, DCM, of the 2nd Royal Welch Fusiliers who had received his gallantry awards while serving as a trooper in the Boer War. In a debate in the House of Commons on 18 January 2006 (Hansard), Keith Simpson, MP, recalled that Captain Dunn, who went on to serve as a medical officer on the Western Front, had published his diaries, in which he had expressed his views on morale and discipline. He was one of only two medical officers who gave evidence to the committee. He was a man who was 'absolutely convinced of the deterrent value of executing those who wilfully deserted and absconded; he believed in the deterrent effect', but his choice of the word 'wilfully' suggests that he did not believe it should apply to those men who simply could not help themselves as a result of mental trauma.

Following a strong campaign from abolitionists, such as Ernest Thurtle, MP, who had himself served as a captain on the Western Front, the death penalty for eight offences committed on active service was abolished in 1928. These offences included striking or offering violence to a superior officer, disobeying a lawful order so as to display a wilful defiance of authority, and sleeping or being drunk while on sentry duty. The death penalty remained for desertion, cowardice, leaving a post without orders, mutiny and treachery when committed on active service. Thurtle was an abolitionist because he felt that it was unfair that military law 'enabled non-fighting people, the majority, to send fighting men, the minority, to be killed or maimed in any cause the majority may decide proper. And the fighting man may not refuse on pain of death, or at least, penal servitude.'

He went on to write:

> … in these days no democracy has the right to shoot any man, volunteer or conscript, because he is unable to withstand the horrors of modern war. If war cannot be waged without the Death Penalty, and we take the penalty away, much the worse for the people who make wars but good care no doubt to those who fight in them.

But it was not until April 1930, in the face of considerable opposition in both the House of Commons and the House of Lords, from among others a number of retired senior officers, that the death penalty was finally abolished in the military for all the remaining offences except those of serious misconduct in action, assisting the enemy, obstructing operations, giving false air signals, mutiny or incitement to mutiny, and failure to suppress a mutiny with intent to assist the enemy. The death penalty for these remaining offences was finally abolished in 1998.

Brigadier F.P. Crozier made an interesting, if somewhat confused, contribution to the abolition debate. He seemed to misunderstand the terms 'abolition' and 'reform', and clearly thought that it was the method of execution that needed to be reformed and that the firing squad itself was the focus of abolition. Crozier acknowledged that this needed doing but then, completely missing the intention and purpose of the debate, went on to advocate that the firing squad should be replaced by a single machine gun which he felt would be more efficient. In this, ironically, he was probably correct.

† † †

Military executions in the First World War do not constitute the British Army's finest hour. The conduct of the courts martial themselves has given rise to many concerns around the processes and procedures followed, the lack of suitable legal representation for defendants, and the failure to call relevant witnesses. There are many excellent books available for those who are interested and want to find out more, and so those concerns do not have to be covered again in this book.

It is difficult, though, to move on without restating the part that chance played in the death penalty. Moore (1999) repeats a story told by Major M.M. Wood, MP, in 1921, who said that he had been told by someone who had acted as the president of a court martial that he had always imposed the maximum sentence because he felt secure in the knowledge that there was a confirming officer further up the chain of command who would in the end make the final decision. Unfortunately, a confirming officer subsequently told Wood that he had never commuted a death sentence because he had always felt that the members of the court martial, having seen the prisoner themselves, were in a better position to impose the proper sentence. As a consequence, men would be executed because of such basic misunderstandings.

While the generals were reluctant to see the death penalty abolished for offences committed on active service because they saw such a step having a negative impact on discipline, it is important to note that not a single Australian soldier through-out the First World War was ever sentenced to death by a court martial, despite pressure from Sir Douglas Haig. It would be hard to argue that no Australian soldier ever fell asleep whilst on guard duty or committed any of the other offences but, equally, it would be hard to argue that the lack of the ultimate deterrent affected their ability to perform in the field. This difference in approach was summed up by a British soldier, Private George Morgan, who made the following observation (Brown, 2001): 'They didn't shoot any Australians. They would have rioted. They weren't like us. We were docile.'

Conversely, it should be noted that the French Army exe-cuted about 600 of its men, the Germans forty-eight, and the Belgians thirteen. The German Army was double the size of the British Army and yet executed a much smaller number of its men. So once again, the question needs to be asked – were the German soldiers better disciplined than their British counterparts or was a different approach to these matters adopted?

The death penalty was used to deter those on active service from committing one or more of the proscribed offences. For deterrence to be effective, the sentences needed to be publicised, but there is evidence (Moore, 1999) that this was not always the case and 'some victims … were put to death almost in secret'. Moore felt that at times the army was deliberately secretive about what it was doing and went on to say, 'Certainly, despite pronouncements and promulgations, doubts remained in the minds of many soldiers as to the frequency of executions and the details of the last grim rites.'

† † †

It is also difficult to read about the military's, and in particular the officers', support for the use of the death penalty without concluding that class factors were also at play. At the outbreak of the First World War, British society was very much class-based. By way of an example, military commissions were available for the taking for young men from public schools but not for those from grammar schools (Marr, 2009); however, that had to change as stocks in that particular pond became depleted as casualties mounted. As the need for more officers became pressing, the army's response was to create temporary officers who would hold their commission for the duration of the war but who could only be drawn from the ranks of the sergeants and corporals. These experienced men, however, were very often reluctant to take a commission because they felt that their chances of survival would be less as an officer – junior officers had a life expectancy of just six weeks (Lewis-Stempel, 2011) – despite the attraction of time out of the line for officer training. Nevertheless, by the end of the war it was estimated that 40 per cent of officers came from the lower and middle classes (Paxman, 2013).

Interestingly, and perhaps ^Not surprisingly, there were even bri-
gades and battalions formed that catered solely for those from
the upper and middle classes so that they would not have to
serve alongside men from the lower classes. A further example of the class divide was that letters from the soldiers in
the trenches to their loved ones were subject to censorship,
with their officers reading them and blocking out anything
untoward, while officers were trusted and their letters were
allowed to be sent home without anyone casting an eye over
them. In addition, officers were granted more leave than their
men and this became a source of grievance as the war dragged
on. Officers also had servants and ate better meals than those
of lower rank. It was also true that as an officer you were more
likely to be treated for shell shock, if needed, than the men
you commanded.

This is not in any way a denigration of the officer class per
se, because there is ample evidence of mutual respect between
some men and their officers, nor is it a 'bash the generals' or
a reprise of the 'lions led by donkeys' argument. It is simply
making the point that the lack of equality in treatment of all
combatants is striking and undeniable.

The class system was therefore as much an actuality in the
British Army as it was in British society in general, and this
would not begin to change until after the war ended. The
casualty rate among the upper and middle classes was one
factor in this change, as, for example, the Oxbridge colleges
suffered twice the national average of deaths, and ducal families suffered more violent deaths in the period 1880–1930 than
during 1330–1479; a period that covered the Hundred Years'
War and the Wars of the Roses (Marr, 2009).

Perhaps of more concern is that up to late 1916 no officer
had been shot for a disciplinary offence, while in the same
period some 154 other ranks were executed (Moore, 1999).
By the end of the war only three officers had been executed,
and one of those was for murder. The officers executed were
Lieutenant Eric S. Poole of the 11th Battalion, West Yorkshire
Regiment, executed on 10 December 1916 (desertion),

The grave of Second Lieutenant E.S. Poole of the West Yorkshire Regiment, one of the few officers to be executed. Eric Poole was born in Nova Scotia. Wounded and shell-shocked on 7 July, he was only declared fit for duty again on 1 September. On 5 October, as his platoon moved up towards the front line at Flers on the Somme, he wandered off. He was found two days later. At his count martial, the man who had passed him fit for duty in September, Lieutenant-Colonel Martin RAMC, was head of the examining medical board. They found that Poole was 'of sound mind' but that 'his mental powers are less than average'. (Courtesy of Paul Kendall)

Sub-Lieutenant Edwin Dyett of the Nelson Battalion, Royal Naval Division, executed on 5 January 1917 (desertion), and Second Lieutenant John Paterson, 3rd Essex Regiment (attached to the 1st), executed on 24 September 1918. Paterson was executed for the murder of a military policeman who challenged him when he was found with his French girlfriend.

Officers were only human and so must have shared the same emotional and physical response to warfare as the men they commanded, so why did the army only feel it necessary to execute such a small number? In fact, it could have executed many more, as those officers found wanting were either sent home or transferred away from the front, while a private soldier would have been placed on a charge. This was despite Sir Douglas Haig commenting in his diary on 6 December 1916, following his confirmation of the death sentence on Lieutenant Eric S. Poole, that desertion by an officer should be treated more severely than with the other ranks. He went on to write that the other ranks needed to know that officers were subject to the same law as them. It is not possible to say whether Sir Douglas Haig would have known the extent to which problematic officers were finessed out of the front line by those further up the chain of command, and although no such scandal ever entered the public domain, this could have been a further factor in the army's coyness over its use of the death penalty.

A further example of this inequality concerns the execution of Private Thomas Highgate, the first soldier to be executed. Highgate had deserted during the retreat from Mons in September 1914, and yet two officers who had tried to surrender their respective battalions during that same retreat were cashiered out of the army. The officers concerned were Lieutenant-Colonel Ellington (Royal Warwickshire Regiment) and Lieutenant-Colonel Mainwaring (2nd Dublin Fusiliers); in fact, some years after the war Mainwaring was restored to his former rank by George V.

Class can also be seen as a factor when some of the comments written in support of confirmation of the death sentence, as the paperwork made its way to the commander-in-chief, were along the lines of 'I consider him to be an insubordinate man of low class'. The Irish Government Report (2004) gives a number of other examples, including: 'The accused is a determined shirker during a time of war and unworthy of being a soldier or Englishman' and 'this man's value as a fighting soldier is NIL'.

As a further example of the inequality of approach, it was also the case that King George V retrospectively pardoned those in the higher ranks, both during and after the war, following petitions and appeals signed by military personnel who had friends who could, it must be assumed, exert significant influence. The Irish government's report in 2004 gave a number of examples of this, including Lieutenant G.D.C. Tracey of the 1/7th Gordon Highlanders who was court-martialled on 11 June 1915 on a charge of cowardice. He was sentenced to be cashiered (which was not an alternative sentence for the lower ranks) but the king granted him an unconditional pardon on 5 December 1923.

This was to be something that those seeking pardons for the men executed would later use to argue that the king had set a precedent, and as the Irish government's report in 2004 stated, 'A military system of law that provides one form of justice to the lower ranked troops on the front line, and another to the officers and upper echelons, cannot be deemed to be just and must be seen for what it evidently was: biased.'

Today we can see the injustice in this, but even allowing for the prevailing standards and norms of the times, this should not have been acceptable then.

† † †

When war broke out in August 1914, Britain had a small but highly trained army and it was those men who made up the British Expeditionary Force, numbering 100,000, that was sent to the Western Front. Field Marshal Earl Kitchener of Khartoum became Secretary of State for War in August 1914, and he realised that the successful prosecution of the war would require large numbers of men to join the army. So he launched a number of appeals in an effort to raise an additional 500,000 men, leading to the production of the 'Your Country Needs You' and other iconic posters from that period. The men were to be raised in tranches of 100,000 and, to facilitate this, recruitment offices were opened across the country.

The men who enlisted had to be a minimum of 19 years of age, yet despite this many underaged youths were still able to join the colours by lying about their age. In addition, they had to pass a medical, accept the King's Shilling and swear an oath of allegiance to the Crown for the duration of the war.

my uncle was 14!

It was this period that saw the clever introduction of the 'pals' battalions', where groups of men from the same town, business or industry were encouraged to join up together. This initiative drew on the romantic notion of friends and colleagues going off to war together, although the romance turned to horror for the communities concerned when so many of the pals' battalions were decimated in July 1916 at the Battle of the Somme. *where he died age 16*

Despite these efforts, and those of the unofficial recruitment officers – the young ladies who gave out their white feathers indiscriminately to anyone not in uniform – the numbers joining up started to decline. The government's response was the National Registration Act in July 1915, which compelled all men between the ages of 15 and 65 to register. By that autumn a further 5 million men of military age had been identified, of whom about 3 million were technically eligible, the difference reflecting those in reserved occupations who had not yet volunteered. In 1916, the Military Services Act introduced conscription: initially for all single men between the ages of 18 and 41, only exempting those in reserved occupations, the disabled, those who could prove that they were the only means of support for dependants, or conscientious objectors – and it would be these men who would go on to form the bulk of the army thereafter. A few months later this was expanded to include married men as well.

There were some 16,000 conscientious objectors in the First World War who refused to fight. Men became conscientious objectors for a variety of reasons, with some viewing themselves as out-and-out pacifists who were against war in general. Some men objected on political grounds, refusing to accept that Germany was their enemy, while others objected on religious grounds; for some it might have been a combination of these reasons. Britain, unlike other countries, had a long tradition of allowing exemption on grounds of conscience, and such men therefore had an opportunity to argue for exemption.

These men had to present themselves before what would inevitably be a hostile tribunal to state their case. This represented a considerable act of bravery in itself on their part, given that the tribunal's starting premise was that they were nothing more than shirkers.

One man who was resolutely opposed to war was Morgan Jones, from Gelligaer in the Rhymney Valley in Wales, who received his call-up papers in early 1916, and stated he was (Hansard, 7 November 2013) 'resolutely opposed to all warfare'. He argued that the war was the result of wrong-headed diplomacy. However, perhaps predictably, the local tribunal concluded that he would not be excluded from military service. He therefore appealed to the tribunal in Cardiff, but his appeal failed. At the same time, action was being taken against the 'No Conscription Fellowship' of which he was a member, and he was found guilty in that regard as well and sent to prison, where he suffered both mental and physical hardship. He was released at the end of the war and stood for Parliament in 1921, becoming the first conscientious objector to be elected as a Member of Parliament.

Some men who came before the tribunals were known as Absolutists, numbering about 1,200 in all, who not only opposed war but also conscription itself, believing that any alternative service that supported the war effort, in effect supported the immoral practice of conscription as well. The tribunals had the power to give these men complete and unconditional exemption.

The conscientious objectors were dealt with in a variety of ways, with about a third being sent to prison. There was one instance in May 1916 (Paxman, 2013) when a number of conscientious objectors were taken to France to be humiliated in front of a battalion of soldiers. Others were sentenced to death with the sentence later commuted to a term in prison.

The government also came up with a number of projects for 'work of national importance', involving forestry or farming, that men were sent to work on. Some conscientious objectors were prepared to serve on the front as members of the Royal Army Medical Corps where they displayed a willingness to work under appalling conditions, and some displayed a level of bravery that was subsequently honoured. Over the course of the war, some 3,000 conscientious objectors served in the Non-combatants Corps (known to the soldiers as the 'No Courage Corps'), where they carried out manual work behind the lines.

It is possible to argue that widespread knowledge on the Home Front of the military executions taking place would not have helped recruitment and would have swelled the numbers seeking exemption, and thereby hindered the fulfilment of the 'basic tenet of military law in that the penalty did nothing to precipitate a manpower shortage'. This could have been a further reason for the lack of transparency on this matter, at least until after conscription was introduced in 1916, which may, in turn, have eased the government's thinking on how families were to be told about their loved ones being executed.

In November 1917 the War Cabinet decided that, as from that moment, the families of those executed were to be informed that their loved ones had died on active service, which had, in any case, been the informal procedure on the part of some commanding officers, despite considerable opposition from the higher echelons of the army. As an example, the service record of Private Highgate, the first man to be executed in 1914, states that he had 'died of wounds', although his medal card states that his medals were 'forfeited for desertion'.

Up until 1917 the Army Record Office, which was dependent on information from the front, had simply and bluntly informed families that their loved one 'was sentenced after trial by court martial to be shot for desertion … and the sentence was duly carried out on …'

The families of the men executed were left devastated, in many cases ashamed, and sometimes ostracised within their communities. The effect on the family of Lance-Corporal Peter Goggins was clearly devastating, as his mother had a breakdown and his wife of six months simply disappeared. The wife of another executed man went to her local post office in 1916 and was met with, 'We don't give pensions to the widows of cowards.' As a result she was left destitute, with a 3-year-old and a 4-month-old child to feed.

The family of Private Bertie McCubbin, of the 17th Sherwood Foresters, was understandably upset to be informed that he had been killed by a 'gunshot'. Unbeknown to the family, he had in fact been executed on 30 July 1916, having been sentenced for cowardice, a fact his mother only discovered after one of his friends returned from the front line and told her the truth. As his niece, Mrs Doris Sloan, recalled, 'she went insane with grief. She never received his medals and never received a pension because he was shot as a coward.'

On occasions, those who returned from the war were prepared to talk about their experiences, and in one village they spoke of the execution of a man with whom they had grown up, gone to school and gone to war. The family itself did not tell people what had happened, but all the other men who returned told their families. The son of the man who had been executed then had to endure the awful experience of going to school with the other boys, many of whom brought in the medals their fathers had won, and then proceeded to give him a hard time. The family was never able to shed the stigma and his mother had great difficulty facing the local community, but because they had no means to move away they had to live with it – for the rest of their lives.

The army raised many objections to the government's proposal, ranging from the issue of the families of those executed receiving benefits and their loved ones' campaign medals, to concerns that such a change would undermine military discipline. An unintended consequence of families being misinformed that a loved one had been killed in action occasionally led to other members of the man's family joining up to seek revenge on the Germans, as recalled by Corporal Alan Bray, whose recollections were discussed earlier. He recalled that the misery of the comrades of the man executed was later made worse when they discovered that the man's father had joined up to fight the Germans to avenge his son, when perhaps those to blame were in fact nearer to home.

It has taken many years for the names of those executed to be added to rolls of honour and memorials up and down the country because feelings still run high in communities on both sides of the debate. A case in point is Fulstow in Lincolnshire, which had never had a memorial to those killed in the First World War because in 1918 the community could not agree on the inclusion of the name of Private Charles Kirman, of the 7th Lincolnshire Regiment, who had been executed on 23 September 1917 for desertion. The issue was so contentious that Fulstow did not have an Armistice Day service until 2005, when finally agreement was reached to place a plaque in the village hall commemorating all those killed in the two world wars, including Private Kirman.

† † †

It is hard to argue that those on the Western Front did not know of the likely consequences of committing certain offences, but there is some evidence that for many it was viewed as something that was more theoretical than a reality, as without proper communication the deterrent nature of the act was simply not getting through. Was this caused by incompetence, negligence, or a deliberate wish to cover it up?

George Coppard of the 6th Queen's Royal West Surrey Regiment (Moore, 1999), according to the diaries that he had written while serving on the Western Front, felt erroneously that in 1917 the army had changed its policy and instead of

executing men had instead sent the condemned on 'danger-
ous patrols or raids', although there is no evidence that this
was the practice. This belief was perhaps reinforced by such
men appearing in the casualty lists as killed in action. If those
serving believed that the death penalty was an empty threat,
then its deterrence aspect was severely undermined, meaning
that some men were being executed simply for the sake of
being executed.

Captain J.C. Dunn, DSO, MC and Bar, DCM (1989) was
the medical officer with the 2nd Battalion of His Majesty's
23rd Foot, The Royal Welch Fusiliers, and his diaries covering
1914–18 on the Western Front do not contain any references
to executions that he either attended or might have known
of. There is, though, an interesting entry for 15 October 1917
where he writes:

> Plainly no action whatever is to be taken against our habit-
> ual deserter, clear as is the evidence of wilfulness if it were
> offered. And yet what use? To gratify a mawkish humani-
> tarianism two or three score mean fellows are encouraged
> to slip away every time there is risk to their skins, so more
> and more average men learn to shirk with impunity; attacks
> fail, and losses run into untold thousands because the most
> dutiful of our men are not backed up.

Dunn eloquently makes the case for the use of the death penalty, and his frustration at the implications of not using it comes
across very clearly. In contrast Plowman (2001) shows a different perspective on desertion: 'I understand desertion. A man
distraught determines that the last act of his life shall at least
be one of his own volition; and who can say that what is com-
monly regarded as the limit of cowardice is not then heroic?'

In addition, Lieutenant-Colonel Meyler, who became MP
for Blackpool and was subsequently to speak up in support
of Ernest Thurtle, made the point: 'You train your soldiers
not to be impressed by fear, to despise fear, and then you go
and bring out ... this death sentence which is supposed to

improve their discipline by means of fear. The whole thing is illogical.' (Moore)

Meyler, therefore, believed that the use of the death penalty was illogical, and this was a view that Thurtle also shared when he wrote that the War Office, as a last resort, had defended the death penalty on the grounds of military necessity. He interpreted this as demonstrating that it was only the threat of being shot by men of their own side that kept the British soldier fighting, even though, as he pointed out, the death penalty had not applied to the Australian soldiers.

† † †

There was obviously some disquiet within the British Army and among politicians, because after the war, papers detailing the proceedings of court martial where the death penalty was imposed, were deemed to be so secret that they were not to be released for 100 years. In the end, this embargo was lifted after seventy-five years, after the names of those shot had been made public in the book *Shot at Dawn*. As a result, it was 1990 before families, campaigners and historians had their first opportunity to examine them all. In many ways it is fortunate that they still existed, as an attempt was made in 1972 in the House of Commons by Don Concannon, MP, to have them destroyed. Fortunately, the government of the day disagreed and Geoffrey Johnson Smith, the Minister of State for Defence, stressed the need to balance protection of the individual from unnecessary pain, and recognition that they constituted important historical documents.

With those condemned to death already dealt with, it could be assumed that 'the protection of the individual' referred to above related to their families, curiously seeking to protect them from something that many, if not all, were already aware of. It is interesting to speculate that the protection of the individual perhaps instead referred to those who had participated in the court martial, as their names were stated on the official papers, and the concern was more likely to be that they could have been subject to some form of retribution, both physical and legal, from the families and friends of those executed.

One of the first casualties of war is truth, as the military and the politicians seek, for a variety of reasons, to control the type and flow of information made available to the public. This is as true today as it was 100 years ago – Iraq and the weapons of mass destruction being a recent example of this, and over time some of those reasons seem more indefensible. The First World War was fought in a time when the actions of politicians were not subjected to the same degree of scrutiny that, quite rightly, is the norm today. The flow of news was strictly controlled – not the case today with twenty-four-hour news coverage and embedded journalists – and so the public remained largely unaware of the numbers of men being executed and the manner of their deaths.

As discussed earlier, a search of the battalion/regiment diaries of those executed, held at The National Archives, was striking in that they do not appear to contain any references to these events. Putkowski and Sykes (1996) wrote about the practice of 'weeding', or redacting as it is now called, where, prior to the release of material relating to court martial or disciplinary matters, information was removed to 'thwart the inquisitive'. This immediately leads to the question – what was there to hide?

In the years after the war, the army was challenged on a number of occasions to reveal court papers where the death penalty had been enacted, but had argued that it could not do this because, under section 124 of the Army Act, only the condemned man was entitled to obtain a copy of the court proceedings, and as they were dead then that constituted an end to the matter. This precluded the families of those shot, the abolitionists and Members of Parliament from gaining access to the papers, and again the question has to be asked – why? What was there to hide? It is only possible to conclude that the politicians must have colluded with the military, because it would have been well within their powers to have changed this nonsensical situation.

The British Army, in the form of its senior officers, desperately wanted to retain the death penalty and argued against its abolition, and yet, despite the bullish comments of ex-officers in Parliament, it appeared in some way embarrassed and wanted to hide what went on from the civilian population. The British Army might have been further embarrassed by the fact that the executions appear to have been unregulated and subject to the proclivities of individual commanding officers.

On the basis of the evidence gathered, the abolition of the death penalty in the military was justified, and it is certainly the case that the actions of the military hierarchy and a number of politicians appear to be questionable. Furthermore, there was to be a long campaign to obtain pardons for those executed, excluding those shot for murder or mutiny.

8

THE CAMPAIGN
FOR PARDONS FOR
THOSE EXECUTED

In 1983, the Lord Chancellor's Department had allowed Judge Anthony Babington to read the surviving courts martial papers. This resulted in his book *For the Sake of Example, Capital Courts Martial 1914–18: The Truth* being published in 1983. Babington was critical of both the secrecy involved and the conduct of the courts martial, but he did not name the men shot. The book was a success and demonstrated the public interest in this aspect of the First World War.

The question of whether the men who had been executed should be pardoned divided opinion as the country approached the last decade of the twentieth century, and it still does to this day. The campaign to obtain pardons really took off with the publication of Putkowski and Sykes' book *Shot at Dawn* in 1989, as this was the first publication to enter the public domain that named the men who had been executed and which also called for the exoneration of 'all 351 men executed by the British Army in the First World War'. While this book could be viewed as central to the subsequent campaign, it unwittingly made the first of two mistakes that were to provide ammunition to those opposed to the granting of pardons. The figure of 351 men included the thirty-seven men who had been found guilty of murder and had, therefore, received the same sentence

that they would have in the civilian world. Those opposed to
the granting of pardons seized on this and made it a central part
of their case; in arguing against murderers being pardoned, they
sought to stop the others being pardoned as well. The book's
second mistake will be discussed later.

The campaign for those executed to receive pardons rested
on a triumvirate of three people – Julian Putkowski, Andrew
Mackinlay and John Hipkin – working in harness. Mackinlay
acted as the spearhead in Parliament, Hipkin campaigned outside Parliament and Putkowski provided them both with the
details of those executed.

The Shot at Dawn campaign was organised by John Hipkin,
a retired Newcastle school teacher, in the early 1990s to fight
for pardons for the men who had been executed in the First
World War, and it was to prove to be a highly effective single-
issue pressure group. Hipkin himself was particularly concerned
with the executions of soldiers who were underage, both at
the time of their enlistment and their death, and he had been
particularly moved by the case of Private Herbert Burden of
the 1st South Northumberland Fusiliers. Private Burden had
lied about his age and had joined up when only 16 years of
age, and on 21 July 1915 he was executed, having been found
guilty of desertion. At the time of his death he was still only 17
and therefore too young to be officially in his regiment. John
Hipkin said, 'I couldn't believe it was true, but when I looked
into it there were others, and this really angered me.'

For sixteen years John Hipkin and his supporters carried
on with the campaign, tirelessly writing to many politicians, as
well as the Queen, coordinating leaflet campaigns and public
meetings. John Hipkin became a familiar figure at political and
other gatherings around the country, standing silently with his
protest placard; he attended meetings at home and abroad. He
was arrested on a number of occasions, unjustly in the eyes of
his supporters, and was nicknamed the 'Silent Protestor' as he
stood quietly with his placard whenever and wherever he felt
he could make an impact; in expectation of arrest, he always
had an overnight bag with him. On 9 November 1997, his own

forty-third wedding anniversary, John Hipkin was arrested for trespass when he displayed a placard in Westminster Abbey's garden of remembrance demanding pardons for those executed. He was taken to Charing Cross police station and released after twenty minutes, but not before he had been threatened with a night in the cells if he returned to Westminster Abbey.

John Hipkin explained what motivated him to start his campaign:

> I still find it very difficult to believe that the British Army would order its officers to shoot boys of 17. Boys who were patriotic enough to fight for Britain and boys that should have been sent home. That's what I'm fighting for. I'm fighting for the boys … *I* was brought up to believe that officers were gentlemen. We were almost brainwashed to respect the Empire. But gentlemen do not shoot boy soldiers.

The Shot at Dawn campaigners were frustrated because some politicians – especially those who were in opposition at the time – promised help, only to change their minds after gaining power. In 1992, the Labour MP for Thurrock, Andrew Mackinlay, became interested in the campaign and wrote to the then prime minister, John Major, who replied, 'We are able to learn from history and the experiences of earlier generations but I think it would be wrong to try and rewrite the events of the past to accord with modern philosophies and outlook.'

As the Conservative government could not be stirred into action, Mackinlay moved a Private Members Bill in 1993, which sought to 'provide for the granting of pardons to soldiers of the British Empire forces executed during the Great War of 1914 to 1919'. Mackinlay's bill, however, did not include provision for pardoning those executed for murder or mutiny but sought to have a tribunal consisting of three judges set up to review, report and make a recommendation as to a pardon on the remaining cases. The content of the bill would have been welcomed to varying degrees by both sides of the debate, but it went further by seeking to provide for compensation to

The Journal   Monday, June 18, 2001

Permanent reminder of a terrible injustice

ON Election morning, photographers and reporters from the nation's media organisations gathered in a Sedgefield meadow to watch local Labour Party candidate Tony Blair striding across a field with his family to vote in a nearby polling station.

Just out of view, shepherded away by Labour Party officials, was John Hipkin, 74, from Walkergate, Newcastle, carrying a placard in the 11th year of his Shot at Dawn campaign. He did not get to speak to Mr Blair.

The pensioner's quest for justice started 10 years ago after reading of the 306 British men and boys who were sentenced to die at the hands of their comrades during the First World War.

In December 1990, *The Journal* published the names of the Northumberland Fusiliers and Durham Light Infantry men who were executed for battlefield offences, after the Government lifted a 75-year-old cloak of secrecy surrounding the circumstances of their deaths.

Mr Hipkin has travelled throughout the country to bring attention to the Shot at Dawn campaign. He has twice confronted Mr Blair to demand an explanation of his Government's position on the issue.

"We are still looking for pardons, but the opening of this memorial is a great step forward in the campaign because there is no other war memorial like this anywhere in the world," Mr Hipkin said.

The statue to be unveiled at the National Memorial Arboretum near Lichfield, Staffordshire is modelled on Northumberland Fusilier Herbert Burden who was just 17 when he was put in front of a firing squad as punishment for desertion.

The 10-foot high sculpture will be surrounded by 306 stakes representing the soldiers who were killed by firing squads for battlefield offences.

Pte Burden had left his battalion to comfort a friend who had lost a brother in the war. He was executed as an example to others.

In a short hearing the commanding officer on the judging panel, Brigadier General Douglas Smith said: "There are a few cases of desertion and the death penalty is the only way it can be stopped."

Pardons campaign: Newcastle pensioner John Hipkin with sculptor Andrew De Comyn's maquette of the statue, based on Northumberland Fusilier Pte Herbert Burden. The full-size statue will be unveiled on Thursday. Below: Pte William B Nelson of the Durham Light Infantry who was one of the 306 soldiers shot at dawn for battlefield offences.

A statue, based on a Northumberland Fusilier, marking the plight of First World War soldiers shot for cowardice and desertion is to be unveiled on Thursday. **Graeme King** spoke to Newcastle man John Hipkin about his campaign to have those soldiers pardoned.

John Hipkin in June 2001, shortly before the unveiling of the statue of Northumberland Fusilier Herbert Burden, who was shot at the age of 17. The statue is at the National Memorial Arboretum (see image opposite). John Hipkin holds a model of the 10ft-high sculpture.

be paid at the discretion of the Secretary of State on a case-by-case basis.

A Private Members Bill is never likely to be passed unless it is supported by the government, and this one was to be no different, as was the case with an Early Day Motion (No.53) tabled on 23 November 1993, which asked:

> That this House calls upon the Government to issue pardons to those men executed by firing squad during the First World War, many murdered at the orders of their own officers, without proper trial or defence, despite being shell shocked or otherwise mentally ill, thereby removing the unfair shame and stigma suffered by their families even to this day.

This Early Day Motion attracted eighty-one signatures, mainly from Labour MPs, and was followed by another Early Day Motion on 30 November 1994 (No.154), which asked:

> That this House calls upon the Prime Minister to posthumously pardon those United Kingdom citizens executed in the First World War on orders of officers who often failed to observe the Army Act; and notes that some citizens were

obscenely executed in abattoirs to the permanent disgrace of this country and its officer corps.

It attracted forty-five signatures, mainly from Labour MPs again, with no support once more from the Conservatives.

On 13 December 1995, Andrew Mackinlay rose to his feet in the House of Commons to raise once more the issue of pardons for those who had been executed in the First World War, on the grounds that:

The men were not given the opportunity to prepare an adequate defence. Many of them were not represented at all; if they were represented, it was by somebody who was demonstrably not qualified to do so. After their field court martial were completed, they were often not told what their sentence was until between 12 to 24 hours before it was carried out. Not only is that demonstrably unfair and unjust, but for all the 300-plus soldiers, there was no right of appeal against the sentence of death.

In what turned out to be another futile attempt to change the Conservative government's mind, he added:

My postbag shows beyond all doubt that, in a sense, those men have been pardoned by the highest court in the land – British public opinion. If one discusses the matter with people in our streets and in clubs among ex-service men and women who went through the first and second world wars, and with serving service men and women today, one finds that, overwhelmingly, they proclaim that those men were brave British soldiers who should be granted pardons. I hope for and look forward to the support not only of Opposition Members but of the many Conservative Members who have over the months told me of their support for such pardons to be granted.

In 1995, the office of Tony Blair, the leader of the opposition, perhaps with a willingness at that stage still to embrace populist views, issued a statement giving an undertaking that a future Labour government would look sympathetically at this matter. It seems clear, judging by what later transpired, that the statement was made before any documentation had been looked at or legal advice sought.

In a debate in the House of Commons on 9 May 1996, the Conservative government's position was outlined as follows:

> The rules that applied during the first world war differ from those now governing the conduct of courts martial. However, these soldiers were convicted by a properly constituted court, according to the laws and procedures of the land, of an offence punishable by the imposition of the death penalty. That we do things differently today cannot alter the fact, uncomfortable as it might be for many of us.

Andrew Mackinlay replied:

> The principles of English law, that people should have a fair trial, be able to prepare a defence and be able to appeal against sentence, were not invented after 1918. They are the basic principles of English law since long before, and were denied to those men in our century.

An amendment to the Armed Forces Bill, which would have secured pardons for those executed in the First World War, was defeated by 203 votes to 129. Among the Labour opposition who voted in support of the amendment were Dr John Reid, Douglas Henderson and John Spellar, and all three went on to become armed forces ministers after 1997.

Understandably therefore, the Shot at Dawn campaign had high expectations of the Labour government that was elected in 1997, and initially were not disappointed when a review was carried out, and an announcement stated:

> For some of our soldiers and their families, however, there has been neither glory nor remembrance. Just over 300 of

them died at the hands not of the enemy, but of firing squads
from their own side. They were shot at dawn, stigmatised
and condemned – a few as cowards, most as deserters. The
nature of those deaths and the circumstances surrounding
them have long been a matter of contention. Therefore,
last May, I said that we would look again at their cases. The
review has been a long and complicated process. (Official
Report 24 July 1998;Vol. 316, c. 1372.)

But disappointment followed as Dr John Reid, the armed forces
minister, announced in July 1998 (see Appendix 1) that he could
not agree to the granting of any blanket pardons, something
which the Shot at Dawn campaign had in fact never asked for,
as claimed by those who opposed its objective. It had become
apparent to Dr Reid from the courts martial papers that he had
read – and he claimed to have read over half of those available –
that many of those concerned had in fact been guilty based on
the standards and practices that existed at the time of the First
World War. Dr Reid explained in 2009: 'I was told on the highest legal advice at the time – I can say that now that I am not a
Minister – that I could not give a legal pardon' (Hansard).

Dr Reid had also consulted widely in arriving at his
decision, including having a meeting with Judge Anthony
Babington and Julian Putkowski (Hansard, 20 March 1998).
One problem that Dr Reid and his advisers encountered was
the variation in the courts martial papers available to them, as
some were quite comprehensive while others consisted of just
one sheet of paper, and they were handwritten.

In making his announcement, he expressed his regret for all
those killed in the First World War, whether by the enemy or
by execution. His decision was based on concerns that the passage of time caused the grounds for a blanket pardon, on the
basis of their unsafe conviction, to be non-existent because no
new evidence could be presented and no new witnesses could
be forthcoming. He concluded that, as a result, any review would
leave a significant number of the men re-condemned again
because any judgement made had to be based on evidence rather

than belief. There is no doubt that, had he felt able to agree to the granting of pardons, he would have done so – as evidenced by his interest in the matter, the support he gave in the House of Commons in 2006, and the explanation that he gave in 2009.

Therefore, in 1998, the Labour government, which in opposition had appeared to support the campaign, decided that it could not issue a blanket pardon because it was unable to 'distinguish between those who deliberately let down their country and their comrades and those who were not guilty of desertion or cowardice'. Keith Simpson, MP, was a newly appointed junior front bench defence spokesman when he had to respond to Dr Reid's statement, but in a debate on 18 January 2006 he shed some light on to the position in the 1970s when he said:

> It is interesting that, in the 1970s, a large number of Labour Members then in opposition felt very strongly that the then Conservative Government and previous Labour Governments had been far too secretive about the records relating to the men executed and that the likelihood was that there had been a cover-up.

If the Ministry of Defence had hoped that Dr Reid's statement would be the end of the matter, it was to be disappointed because, dismayed but not deterred, the Shot at Dawn campaign kept pressing its case and Andrew MacKinlay said, 'I am deeply disappointed that the Government still refuses to grant pardons but these people have already been pardoned by the highest court in the land, British public opinion' (*Daily Telegraph*, 22 June 2001).

Opponents of the campaign continued to argue about the futility of changing history and that a focus on those executed did a disservice to those killed and wounded in the First World War. But Dr Reid was given cause to reconsider this decision as he explained in 2009 (Hansard):

> During the interval between being Armed Forces Minister and being Secretary of State, I discovered that

New Zealand had apparently managed to accomplish that which I had been told was impossible in Britain. Naturally, and in my normal delicate fashion, I interviewed some of my officials who were still there about why that which we had found impossible had been found possible elsewhere. We re-opened the inquiry, and I am glad to say that my successor, my right hon. Friend the Member for Kilmarnock and Loudoun [Des Browne], did a great deal of work on the matter as Defence Secretary. The result is as is known.

The Shot at Dawn campaign was not daunted and continued to argue for pardons, with a particular focus on the cases of the underage soldiers. It is a further disturbing thought that, in the same way that some of those executed were below the age of 19, having joined up when they were below the minimum age, it is also likely that some of those in the firing squads would have been under the age of 16 as well.

On 16 September 1915, Brigadier-General F.G. Anley, who commanded the 4th Division, issued routine orders that showed that the army was already aware of the problem of underage soldiers and its attitude to the problem. The orders state: 'Lads who are under 17 years of age, according to their birth certificate, which should be produced, will be sent to England unless they are passed fit for service and wish to remain at the front.' This statement is interesting because it made it a condition of repatriation that the 'lad', who was already at the front, had to produce a birth certificate – how many were likely to have this document with them in a legible state after service in a trench? The production of a birth certificate was not something the army had required as a condition of enlistment.

The Ministry of Defence's head of Army Historical Branch, Miss A.J. Ward, OBE, made the ministry's position clear on the execution of underage soldiers in a letter dated 24 March 1999 to John Hipkin:

You also mention that a number of soldiers who were under age were illegally tried and executed. I am afraid this is not the case. Anyone over the age of 14 was deemed legally responsible for his actions, and Army regulations provided no immunity from Military Law for an underage soldier. While measures were taken to remove under age soldiers from the front line when their ages were discovered, anyone who had voluntarily placed himself – albeit through fraudulent enlistment – under Military Law, could not exempt himself from the legal consequences of doing so. John Reid (Secretary of State) paid particular attention in his review to the views, and representations which you, the veterans, and especially the families of those executed made to him. He also consulted and took advice from a number of people outside the Ministry of Defence on historical, legal, and medical aspects of the matter.

In effect, the Ministry of Defence's position was that underage soldiers who had given a false age when enlisting had willingly placed themselves under military law, which stipulated the age of criminal responsibility as 14. This meant that desertion by any serviceman, including those who were technically underage, was correctly punishable by death if so directed by a court martial. The letter also sought to clarify the reasons for the embargo of the courts martial records: namely to 'safeguard the privacy of individual servicemen and their families', which has been discussed elsewhere in this book.

It is debatable whether such a response would have satisfied many people in the immediate aftermath of the war, let alone in more recent times. It certainly did not satisfy an embittered and frustrated John Hipkin, who wrote to David Lewis, a fellow campaigner, regarding the court martial and execution of Private Joseph Byers of the 1st Royal Scots Fusiliers, who had been found guilty of attempting to desert on 8 January 1915. Byers had been arrested on 18 January 1915 and brought before a court martial, where he was found guilty and subsequently executed on 6 February 1915:

Dear David,

Now that the 79 day air war against Yugoslavia has ended, perhaps Mr Blair can turn compassionately to the 79 day war of Fusilier Joseph Byers, the first Kitchener volunteer to be shot at dawn – a patriotic boy aged 16 years and 4 months on 6/2/1915, and his court martial papers kept secret for 75 years.

Fusilier Byers lied about his age to enlist on Nov. 20th, 1914, was shipped to France on Dec. 5th.1914, after only 2 weeks basic training, was later charged with desertion, (a military capital offence abolished by Parliament in 1929) and as an under aged soldier was illegally executed, drugged or drunk, by a reluctant firing squad made up of his own comrades.

The Officers of his court martial received a letter from Gen. Sir Horace Smith-Dorrien commander of 2nd Army dated 2/1/1915 (Public Records Office WO71/397), stating [*sic*] would urge that discipline in the 1st. Batt. Royal Scots Fusiliers had been very bad for some time past and that a severe example is very much wanted. Byers after 79 days in the army was shot at dawn 6/2/1915.

Fusilier Byers like most soldiers was undefended, and like all defendants was not allowed to see what had been written about him. Most court martial officers were without any legal training, and were in fact Judge and Jury. No appeals were allowed.

Pardons for these boys and 303 adolescent and adult soldiers were blocked in parliament in 1996, 1998, and 1999 by both Lab. and Con. Governments.

There are a number of disturbing aspects to this case. Firstly, at his court martial, Private Byers entered a plea of 'guilty' and therefore according to military law the court could not consider any evidence or mitigation – it was in effect a one-word suicide note. Why did Private Byers plead guilty? It was probably a combination of poor or non-existent legal representation, and ignorance (although on the same day, before the same court martial, Private Andrew Evans of the same regiment had already been sentenced to death for desertion).

Some people might say that Private Byers pleaded guilty to perhaps incomprehensibly hide his age because it was for many years believed that he was under 17 years of age when he was executed – when in fact this was not the case (Linklater, 2014).

Private Byers had been wrongly identified by Putkowski and Sykes in their book *Shot at Dawn* as the youngest soldier to be executed. This was the second mistake referred to earlier: an embarrassment that provided further ammunition to those who opposed the Shot at Dawn campaign for pardons, and argued that it highlighted the problems of attempting to rewrite the history books.

This development was a potentially devastating body blow for the campaign. Immediately, John Hipkin had no alternative but to destroy some 3,000 leaflets that had featured a photograph of Private Byers and prominently featured the fact that he had been shot whilst only 16 years of age. Embarrassingly, his face was also on campaign placards, on in-memoriam notices in newspapers, on wreaths laid at the Cenotaph, and in lobbying material sent to Members of Parliament, making him literally the poster boy of the campaign (Linklater). Fortunately, this did not derail the campaign and it continued to 'argue general principle of the injustice of the executions is more important than individual cases'.

The Shot at Dawn campaign continued to make progress, gaining the support of the Royal British Legion. There had been just a solitary dissenting vote when the Royal British Legion supported a call for a pardon for all officers and men sentenced to death for desertion and cowardice in the First World War, believing that a general amnesty or exoneration to mark the new millennium would remove the burden of shame, guilt, and resentment from the families of those executed. In November 2000, an important psychological threshold was crossed when the relatives of those executed were allowed to participate in the Remembrance Day ceremonies at the Cenotaph. The Shot at Dawn campaign was initially only offered five tickets for the march, though this was increased to fifty after some lengthy telephone calls to the Royal British Legion. For the 2001 ceremony the ticket allocation rose to 110 and remained at that level until the pardons were granted.

As the families of those executed took their place in the November 2000 procession, they would have been struck by the irony (some would say insensitivity) of being told to assemble alongside the statue of Field Marshal Sir Douglas Haig (later Earl Haig), the man who had confirmed the death sentences for many of their relatives. At the end of the ceremony the families were informed by reporters that Secretary of Defence Geoff Hoon had announced that it would not be appropriate retrospectively to pardon those executed. The news reduced many to tears.

The British government's opposition to the granting of pardons was undermined when, in 1999, the New Zealand Labour Party was elected into office and the new prime minister, Helen Clark, announced in April 2000 that: 'our conscience wouldn't rest if we didn't do something to retrospectively pardon those soldiers … It's just so pitiful that men who were sick, drunk, epileptic, shellshocked ended up being executed.'

In 2000, the New Zealand Parliament considered the Peck Bill, as it was known; the bill proceeded through Parliament (the vote was 112 in favour with 8 against) and received royal assent as the Pardon for Soldiers of the Great War Act on 14 September 2000. Five New Zealand soldiers who had been executed were granted an unconditional retrospective pardon. In July 2005, the New Zealand prime minister presented the relatives of those soldiers with any outstanding medals, decorations and certificates. Interestingly, in December 2001, the Canadian government issued a formal apology to the families of the twenty-three Canadians who had been executed, but stopped short of granting statutory pardons 'because there is no mechanism for granting them' – despite the actions of New Zealand.

This meant that in three countries, the United Kingdom, New Zealand and Canada, there were three different approaches to dealing with this issue, despite the men having been executed under the same British Army Act of 1914 and in the same war. In Britain there had been neither an apology nor a pardon, although there had been a motion of regret, which it could be argued was as near as possible to an apology; in New Zealand there had been a complete apology and a restitution of all civil rights, and the Canadian government had made an apology, but had not granted a statutory pardon.

† † †

The campaign for pardons continued, and on 17 January 2002, Robin Cook, the leader of the Commons, in response to a request to bring the issue back to the House once again said:

> I am well aware of the strength of feeling of the relatives of those who were shot. I think everybody in the House would express great sympathy with their position and concern about the action that was taken at the start of the last century. It is plain now, in retrospect, that many of those who were sentenced and executed at the time would never have been sentenced or executed under modern law or standards. However, as the hon. Gentleman will know from previous exchanges, there is a bona fide issue as to whether it is credible to apply a legal pardon posthumously in very different circumstances – including the state of the law – from those that applied at the time. Nor would this be the only occasion when we might be invited to do so. Therefore, what I can say to the hon. Gentleman is that he should offer comfort to relatives by telling them of the very strong sympathy and regrets of all of us who are alive today about what happened. However, it is not really for us to make legal judgements by today's standards about what happened 100 years ago.

As Robin Cook made that response he might have had some inkling of what was happening in New Zealand where the proposed Act had received its second reading and been referred to the Foreign Affairs, Defence and Trade Committee.

In October 2004, the Irish government formally submitted to the United Kingdom government a report, 'The Court Martial and Execution of Twenty Six Irish soldiers by the British Army during World War 1', seeking a pardon for the twenty-six men concerned.

In May 2005, a case was brought before the High Court by the family of Private Harry Farr, seeking a full posthumous pardon. It was brought in the name of his daughter, who was aged 92, but the case was adjourned while the Ministry of Defence considered further submissions by the family. Private Farr of the 1st West Yorkshire Regiment had been executed on 18 October 1916, having been found guilty of cowardice.

In November 2005, Andrew Mackinlay, MP, introduced a new version of his Private Member's Bill, which he had introduced in 1993, seeking a pardon for soldiers of the Great War, but this was again unsuccessful.

Keith Simpson, MP, in the Commons debate of 18 January 2006, raised a number of important questions: Had anything changed since 1998? Had the Ministry of Defence been able to find any official documents relating to the courts martial and execution of British soldiers? Had the government's legal opinion changed? Had any new evidence come to light? And had any of the files relating to those who had been sentenced to death but subsequently reprieved been found? This last point was important because those documents would have provided something against which to compare and contrast the documents in respect of those executed, and given valuable information for the grounds of the reprieves granted.

The government responded that no new documents had been found or been forthcoming from other sources, no files concerned with those who had been reprieved had been found, and that its legal position had not changed.

There were still many historians, amongst others, who continued to argue against the granting of pardons because it would effectively be changing history, as the above discussion of the case of Private Byers shows. Lord Ashdown summed up the concerns of those opposing pardons on 12 October 2006:

> … could create precedents for the future and it cannot but have the effect of impugning the judgment of the people who made those very difficult decisions at the time. It cannot but have the effect of revisiting history, which is very dangerous, and putting the gloss and judgments of today on decisions made in conditions which we cannot in our time and at this distance make proper judgments about. (Official Report, House of Lords, 12 October 2006; Vol. 685, c. 430.)

The commander-in-chief, Field Marshal Sir Douglas Haig, will forever be associated with the prosecution of the war on the Western Front and the military executions, so it is perhaps no surprise that his son, George Haig, also opposed the granting of pardons. He claimed that many of those executed were rogues and criminals who deserved to be shot. His view was that history should not be tampered with and the decisions of the army commanders at the time should be respected as they knew best.

Nevertheless, in August 2006, the campaign finally achieved its objective when the Labour government changed its mind and the then Secretary of State for Defence, Des Browne, who had been more sympathetic to the arguments put forward, announced on 16 August that with Parliament's support there would be a general pardon for those executed in the First World War. His intentions were set out in a written ministerial statement on 18 September 2006, which is reproduced as Appendix 2. The written statement acknowledged the exceptional circumstances that had led to the executions and the ongoing stigma that had remained for the families of those concerned. As a result, the government was to seek a statutory pardon for those executed as a group because the variability of the records available made individual pardons difficult and could have left some individual cases failing to meet the criteria for a pardon due to a lack of evidence.

Subsequently, a new law was passed on 8 November 2006, which was included as part of the Armed Forces Act, pardoning the men of the British and Commonwealth armies who were executed in the First World War between 4 August 1914 and 11 November 1918, for all offences except murder and mutiny, thereby removing the stain of dishonour with regard to executions from their war records. However, it did not cancel the actual convictions.

The measure, when debated, still had its opponents in the House, and some were critical of the speed with which the new secretary of state had changed the government's opinion and questioned what precisely this change was based on. One MP reminded the House of Commons in the debate on 7 November 2006 what Dr John Reid had said back in 1998, 'However frustrating, the passage of time means that the grounds for a blanket legal pardon on the basis of unsafe conviction just do not exist. We have therefore considered the cases individually.' (Official Report, 24 July 1998; Vol. 316, c. 1372.)

Others were critical of the decision being made by those they saw as having had no direct military experience themselves. Their concern was that this Labour government lacked direct experience of military life, which had not been the case with its predecessors over the previous fifty years. Some MPs, while supporting the principle of granting a pardon, took issue with the pardons being restricted to those executed rather than to all who had been sentenced to death as they felt that the problem was the conviction rather than the sentence. Their argument was that, as one MP put it:

If I were a member of one of the families concerned who thought that my ancestor had been wrongly convicted because, for example, he had had shell shock, it would not encourage me to know that his conviction stood and he was being pardoned only because of the severity of the sentence, not because of the injustice of the conviction.

In answer to these questions the government said:

> The Ministry of Defence was aware of the views of a number of historians and other interested academics when undertaking its review of this issue. We have also taken account of the views of key interested parties both within Government and more widely, notably the Governments of those countries which are successor states to colonies and dominions from which individuals were executed.

It was also made clear that the government had no plans to extend the pardons to those soldiers convicted of capital crimes but not executed, or to those executed for crimes such as murder and treason.

The outcome in the House of Commons had been by no means certain, and the frustrations of those who sought a remedy for the issue of the executions were summed up by Andrew Mackinlay when he said:

> During World War One, attempts were made by people like myself in Parliament to raise these executions. They were slapped down and suppressed. There was no candour or debate. The argument was advanced – it had some legitimacy – that the country was in the middle of a conflict. Come the 1920s, the matter was raised by several hon. Members, one of whom was Ernest Thurtle, the Member for Shoreditch. He was slapped down and told that he was wrong.
>
> The point that cannot be escaped is that for 75 years it suited the British establishment to suppress the documentation relating to these cases. Now that the documents have become available to families, jurors, politicians and journalists and we see how flawed the trials were, people say, 'It is too late; it is a matter of history.' How very convenient.

Nevertheless, following the passing of the Act, each file was amended to include the conditional pardon granted under section 359 of the Armed Forces Act of 2006, which had

been signed by the Secretary of State for Defence. The file for
Private Thomas Highgate, the first soldier to be executed, had
a note attached which read that the pardon was 'as recognition
that he was one of the victims of the First World War and that
execution was not a fate he deserved'.

As Browne said:

> I believe it is better to acknowledge that injustices were
> clearly done in some cases – even if we cannot say which –
> and to acknowledge that all these men were victims of war.
> I hope that pardoning these men will finally remove the
> stigma with which their families have lived for years.

† † †

Returning to the case of Private Byers, whatever his age
might have been, General Sir Horace Smith-Dorrien, commanding the Second Army, approved the sentence, adding the
note 'deserving of the full penalty' on the grounds that 'discipline in the 1st Battalion Royal Scots Fusiliers has been very
bad for some time past and I think a severe example is very
much wanted'. However, this particular case did seem to give
Smith-Dorrien some pause for thought because he went on
to write, 'by pleading guilty he had made it impossible for regulations to permit the taking of sworn evidence … although
this is legally correct it is just a question as to whether when a
death sentence is involved, the court should make men plead
not guilty and take sworn evidence.' (Linklater, 1998) Some
six months before, General Smith-Dorrien had justified the
public nature of Private Highgate's execution by saying that as
a result no further desertions occurred in his division, but he
may have forgotten that by the time he considered the case of
Private Byers.

What these reflections reveal is that even a hard-line commanding officer was beginning to question the processes and
procedures involved. The downside of changing these was
that the trial process would take longer, which the army did

not want, and, therefore, chance and the Alice in Wonderland nature of these things continued and more men undoubtedly died as a result.

† † †

There are still those who consider that pardoning these men was a mistake and, over a century later, the use of the death penalty continues to divide opinion. Some historians argue that such pardons were a mistake and changed nothing because the decision to execute a soldier was taken in the course of a war when commanders were intent on keeping the army united and fighting. Their argument is that such decisions were therefore taken from a moral perspective that would be beyond the understanding of those who had not experienced combat and, therefore, the fact of the matter is that the death penalty for those offences committed on active service were lawful by the law and practices of those times, even if they appear cruel, capricious and wrong-headed now.

A decision to unveil a memorial at the National Memorial Arboretum in Staffordshire in 2001 has further divided opinion, but it nevertheless presents a powerful visual image with its statue depicting the underage soldier, Private Herbert Burden of the Northumberland Fusiliers, who was executed for desertion on 21 July 1915 when still only 17 years of age and therefore too young even to have been at the front.

The statue, some 10ft tall, shows Private Burden standing bare-headed, blindfolded, a disc pinned over his heart and hands tied behind his back, and, judging by the set of his mouth, there seems to be an unmistakeable look of fear on his face. Facing this statue are six trees to signify the firing squad. Around the statue are 306 stakes in memory of those who were executed, the stakes resembling the posts to which the men were tied before being shot. Each stake bears a metal plaque bearing the executed man's name, age, rank and date of death.

The statue, a sculpture by Andy De Comyn, was unveiled by Mrs Gracie Harris, who was just 3 years old when her father, Private Harry Farr, of the 1st West Yorkshire Regiment, was shot for cowardice on 18 October 1916. Mrs Harris had not learnt about the fate of her father until she was 40 years of age, explaining, 'My mother was too ashamed to tell me but it explains a lot of things that made my mother very sad over the years.' She summed up the feelings of the families of those shot, and those who still campaigned, when she said, 'I am very proud and very grateful that now we have somewhere we can come and pay honour to those soldiers who I consider were wrongly executed.' (*Daily Telegraph*, 22 June 2001)

†††

Even if, 100 years later, the death sentence has to be accepted as being a standard of that time, there are no conceivable grounds for accepting the variation in practice where the actual executions themselves were concerned.

There is something abhorrent yet undeniably logical about the public nature of some of the military executions. Abhorrent because of the nature of the event itself, but logical if the death sentence was ever to be a deterrent to those who might be contemplating desertion.

The natural abhorrence could perhaps be tempered if such executions had had the desired effect of deterring others, but there was no consistency about the British Army's approach to executions, which, as a result, undermined their credibility. There is, therefore, some underpinning logic to General Sir Horace Smith-Dorrien's desire to have Private Highgate publicly executed as a deterrent to desertion, given that he later claimed that there had been no further instances in his division, although it is hard to escape the overall conclusion that the British Army was in fact acting illogically. As Meyler said, military training was about getting soldiers to a point where they were not impressed by fear, and yet the death sentence was meant to improve discipline by causing fear, and there really seems no way to square that particular circle, hence the inevitable conclusion that it was illogical.

The fact that no Australian soldier was ever executed further strengthens the case for the illogicality of military executions, because there is no evidence that Australian soldiers performed less well than their British counterparts as a result. Throughout his time as commander-in-chief, Sir Douglas Haig tried hard to pressure the Australians to adopt the death penalty, but without success. It is impossible to know whether Haig was motivated by principle or by a desire to have the death sentence validated by more nations adopting it. But the Australian opposition to the death penalty stemmed from the case of Breaker Morant, an Australian officer in the Boer War, who had been executed in controversial circumstances. Subsequently, the Australian government made it a condition that none of its soldiers who were to fight in the First World War would be executed.

Furthermore, without a consistent approach to letting soldiers know that executions were taking place, the deterrent impact of the sentence was lost because, at least for some, it was seen as an empty threat. The deterrent aspect of executions was further undermined by the fact that some of those who were eventually shot were repeat offenders, having deserted a number of times. Was it the case that having deserted and been court-martialled, with the sentence then commuted, such men were given the confidence to do it again in the belief that the ultimate sanction would not be imposed?

This leads to the next point: namely, did the British Army and the country's politicians want transparency where executions were concerned? There are a number of strands to this to be considered. Between 1914 and 1916 the army was dependent on volunteers and, therefore, if the extent of death sentences and executions became public knowledge then conceivably this could have affected the numbers of men coming forward to fight. Indeed, the numbers volunteering did in any case start to decline in 1915, leading to conscription, so knowledge of military executions may have exacerbated matters.

Government ministers in the early years of the war were themselves reluctant to admit that men were being executed or to give the numbers involved when questions were asked in Parliament.

Another facet of this lack of transparency was that, up until 1917, the official position was that families would be written to by the Army Records Office and bluntly informed that their family member had been sentenced to death, and that this sentence had been carried out. As a result, the man forfeited all rights to campaign medals and benefits, leaving many families destitute. The Army Records Office could only send such letters if it was informed that a sentence had been carried out, and yet, up until 1917, some commanding officers included those executed in the lists of men killed in action. Were such officers motivated by concerns for the men's families or a desire, for whatever reason, to keep things quiet, thereby protecting themselves and ultimately the army?

The British Army's official stance was that it supported and wanted to keep the death sentence for all the reasons discussed earlier, and yet its actions seem curiously at odds with that. It is interesting, if hugely frustrating, that there is a lack of routine orders where executions are concerned and nothing of note in battalion or regimental diaries due almost certainly to the army's practice of weeding out sensitive documents to defeat the inquisitive. In addition, the papers relating to courts martial proceedings for capital offences were locked away in The National Archives for seventy-five years. The army also refused to hand over the court papers relating to those shot when requested, hiding behind a regulation that only the defendant could ask for such documents and as such men had been shot the army simply refused all requests.

The impression given by the army and the politicians was one of wanting to hide a dark secret and perhaps Mr Clarke was right in claiming that the true figure for the numbers executed was higher than the official figures, although perhaps not as high as he stated.

It is a further unpleasant conclusion that the British class system was indeed a factor where military executions were concerned, despite the sentiments expressed by Sir Douglas Haig in his diary entry. How can it be right that an officer committing a capital offence could be finessed out of the line and sent back to Britain, for instance, and yet a soldier for the same offence could be charged, court-martialled and shot? There can be no defence for the stark statistic that only three officers were ever executed and one of those was for murder. Britain in the early years of the twentieth century was a class-based society and there is an uneasy feeling, based on the sentiments discussed earlier, that the life of an ordinary soldier was valued at somewhat less than that of an officer.

Once again, it is only too easy to see the part that chance played where executions were concerned. As abhorrent as it might be to some, the death sentence was acceptable according to the practices and norms of those times. If, as a result of his actions, a man had committed a capital offence for which he was subsequently found guilty, then the mandatory sentence, subject to any mitigation, would be death and the sentence only carried out following confirmation by the commander-in-chief. Wider issues of discipline and performance by, for example, the man's battalion or regiment should not be allowed to influence whether a man was to be shot or not, and yet such considerations were behind such decisions.

There is something deeply disturbing about this whole subject, even allowing for the norms and practices of those times, but as disturbing as the military executions are, nothing can be done to change the fact that men were shot; undoubtedly the issues can and should be aired and debated if only to achieve greater understanding.

CONCLUSION

Having now considered the roles and experiences of those involved and how executions appear to have been organised on the Western Front, together with the campaigns for the abolition of the death sentence and the campaign for pardons for those executed, it seems appropriate to return to the fictional account that opened this book and to add some additional commentary to explain the background behind what was taking place.

† † †

The condemned man had spent his last night on this earth (*having been informed just a few hours before that his sentence had been confirmed*), in a small room that was barely furnished with a table, two chairs and a straw bed (*the room, an old quarry office, would have been selected and prepared by the APM*). By the light of a guttering candle he had written his final, painful letters to his family and friends and laid out his few personal possessions on the table (*to be passed into the chaplain's safekeeping*). The small room was further diminished in size by the presence of two guards who stood with bayonets fixed by the door and the single window to prevent his escape.

Occasionally through the night, the chaplain came to spend time with him, but otherwise he sat alone with his thoughts. With his letters written he decided that he would spend his last hours awake and so, moving his chair so that he could watch through the window for the approach of dawn, he started on the bottle of rum that had been left on the table (*this had been given to him by the army chaplain*). Inevitably, he fell asleep only to be roused by the sound of footsteps and voices outside the door.

It was just before dawn (*executions were normally carried out at dawn, not for any legal reason but because it was a quiet time with less likelihood of bystanders*) and the sky was starting to get light as a small group of men was marched into an unused quarry. They were then left to stand around smoking and looking anywhere but at each other, not wanting to catch another's eye, the smoke from their cigarettes and pipes drifting upwards to add to the slight mistiness of the morning. Some stared at the ground, some examined their hands, and some stared into the middle distance. Most definitely, nobody wanted to speak, as they all knew what they were there to do. (*The various methods used to select the firing squad were covered in Chapter 3, and so we know now that these men were unfortunate to find themselves in that quarry. It is likely that they had some knowledge of the prisoner and considered the sentence to be harsh.*)

A short distance away stood the lonely figure of the young lieutenant in charge of the firing party, his face pale from the knowledge of what was to come. He smoked ferociously and stamped his feet in an effort to keep warm while he nervously checked and re-checked his service revolver, worried that this morning of all mornings it might jam. (*Lewis-Stempel's book,* Six Weeks: The Short and Gallant Life of the British Officer in the First World War, *reveals that junior officers faced a life expectancy of just six weeks. This young officer, therefore, was facing an additional and unexpected horror that he could never have previously imagined. Perhaps he had sought the comfort of alcohol the night before, or maybe he had been unlucky enough to have been ordered to dine with his commanding officer, who would have been keen to keep him sober.*)

Two companies of the condemned man's regiment then marched (*carrying their full equipment*) silently into the quarry and took up position across its open end, and in response to a shouted order, stood at ease. (*These men had been told to parade in full kit at an ungodly hour to witness this event, a public execution, a practice which had been stopped in civilian life in 1868. Many, if not all, would have felt some sympathy for the prisoner.*)

Soon, too soon for some, they heard the approach of a vehicle and a motor ambulance appeared at the edge of the quarry. The members of the firing squad were called to attention, facing away from the stake (*surrounded at its base by straw to absorb the blood*) that none of them had been able to look at, with their rifles placed on a tarpaulin on the ground behind them.

The condemned man, thankfully very drunk (*he would have been given alcohol and/or some form of sedative by the chaplain or the medical officer; an appropriate question would be to ask whether rendering the prisoner drunk constituted preparing him for a good death, although the effect would have been humane*) and, therefore, apparently senseless as to what was about to happen, was all but carried from the back of the ambulance by two military policemen, accompanied by an army chaplain. The man was so drunk that his arms did not need to be tied behind his back or his legs bound at his ankles as he made the short, stumbling walk to the stake, supported by the military policemen. On arrival at the stake, and held between the two beefy redcaps, his arms were momentarily released before being tied behind it, but being drunk he could not feel the rough surface of the wood against the skin of his wrists and hands. A further binding held his ankles to the stake. As the man drunkenly muttered to himself, a blindfold (*he was required to wear a blindfold not, as many think, to save him from seeing the firing squad, but instead to prevent them from having to look into his eyes; the blindfold might well have been a gas mask that was put on back to front*) was placed over his eyes and the medical officer stepped forward to pin a small, white square of fabric over his heart.

Meanwhile, the lieutenant had loaded a single round of ammunition into each rifle with the help of an assistant provost marshal, and then mixed them up. As was usually the case, one of the rounds was a blank (*we now know that an experienced soldier could tell whether their rifle was the one loaded with a blank by the force of the recoil. It did, though, give some the means of telling themselves, and others if necessary, that they had not fired the fatal shot*). When the rifles were ready, the lieutenant took up his position and signalled to the chaplain to begin saying the condemned man's final prayer. The assistant provost marshal, by a pre-arranged and silent signal, ordered the firing squad to turn, pick up their rifles and prepare to fire, as each worked the bolts of their rifles with trembling hands. At the same time, the watching companies of men were brought to attention. (*All who were present would have been tense, and none more so than the assistant provost marshal and the young lieutenant, who would have known that the firing squad represented the weakest part of the execution process. Would they fire and would they fire accurately?*)

The chaplain solemnly intoned 'Amen' and turned and walked away with his head bowed. The lieutenant then unsheathed his sword and raised it in the air. Fingers tightened on triggers and when the sword was lowered a thunderous volley rang out. Some bullets, whether deliberately or as a result of incompetence, missed the staked figure completely (*some members of the firing squad would have deliberately missed the prisoner, but it is also possible that by having their rifles mixed up they had to use a weapon that was not adjusted to their requirements*) and threw up spurts of dust from the quarry wall behind. Some found their target and the condemned man sagged forward, at which point the medical officer approached him to determine whether life had been extinguished. With a look of disgust, he signalled to the lieutenant that the man was still alive. The lieutenant with a trembling hand then stepped forward to finish him off with a revolver shot through the side of the head.

The watching companies were swiftly marched out of the quarry, with their sergeants silently defying them from looking anywhere but straight ahead. The firing squad was then brought to attention and marched back to its breakfast, also without a sideways glance at the dead man. The firing squad was followed by the lieutenant, the assistant provost marshal, the military policemen and the medical officer, leaving two ambulance bearers to take down the body, which was then wrapped in a cape ready for burial (*the burial site would have been previously identified by the chaplain*), and to clear away the bloodied straw from around the stake. When they were finished, they placed the body on a stretcher and carried it to the burial site where the chaplain presided over a short funeral service.

† † †

I am certain that, scattered around the country, there are individuals, either family members or friends, who will have documents, photographs, recollections or indeed artefacts, but who may not realise their significance in helping to provide a more complete picture of this troubling aspect of the First World War.

By way of an example of this, I was talking to a friend when I was writing this book who told me a story about his family in the First World War. His father had a brother called Jack and a sister, known to everyone as Sis, who Uncle Jack's friend Harold wanted to get to know. Uncle Jack and Harold were sent to the Western Front, but the love-struck young man was desperate to return to London to see the object of his affections for possibly one last time, and so the two of them deserted, probably in about 1916. Somehow they made their way back to London only to be arrested without any hesitation by Uncle Jack's father who was a police sergeant. Remarkably, with duty taking precedence over family ties, he handed over his son and, as it turned out, the man who would be his future son-in-law to the army, knowing full well the penalty for desertion. Despite this, and once again showing the part that chance played, these two lucky young men were returned to France without charges being brought and went on to survive the war, returning safely to their homes in London – which must have made for an interesting family reunion.

I was also able to attend an event at the Royal Shakespeare Theatre in Stratford-upon-Avon in March 2014, when members of the public were invited to bring along artefacts and stories from family members who had served in the First World War. It was incredible to see the wealth of material that people brought along and the stories they had to share, and I am sure others have similar stories. I hope that this book will encourage those people to come forward and share what they know. In doing so, they may be able to help fill in the gaps where this subject is concerned or indeed correct any mistakes or misrepresentations that I may have inadvertently made.

† † †

In my opinion, research will always raise more questions than it answers, particularly when looking at events in the past. Analysis and conclusions must always take account of the standards and practices of those times and this was a point repeatedly made by those who opposed the granting of pardons to the men who had been executed in the First World War. They argued that it was wrong to seek to change history because what had taken place conformed to the procedures of the time, although, in doing so, this appeared to dismiss the long-lasting effect the executions had on families and communities.

However, there is a counter argument: even if the military executions conformed to the standards and practices of the time, society has now moved on, allowing for a reinterpretation of events and improved analysis that means old facts and situations can be viewed through a better prism. Despite that, the analysis that follows will try to adhere to a formula that is based on an acceptance of the practices of the time, but nevertheless has to take the view that what went on was wrong and that the key players should have known that. In fact, as my analysis progresses, there appears to be a case that the key players, and by that I mean the military hierarchy and politicians, did know and this led to their attempts to hide what had taken place.

The procedures of the British Army in the First World War were based on a very detailed set of rules and regulations set out in the annual Army Act, military law and the King's Regulations. My research, although others may subsequently correct me, shows that those rules and regulations seem to peter out once the sentence of death had been confirmed by the commander-in-chief. The notes issued to the army chaplain Edward Guilford in December 1917 are the only detailed example I could find of what might be called a standard operating procedure for the carrying out of an execution, but it has not been possible to establish whether they were meant to apply across the whole army. There are other instructions as to the execution procedure referred to in this book, but they do not contain anywhere near the level of detail contained in the notes to Guilford.

The consequence of this, as the stories of the men who took part in the executions shows, is that there was considerable variation in the way that executions were conducted. The variations identified concern the size of the firing squad, how it was selected, and how the condemned man's last moments were managed. Even allowing for the customs of the times, when the British Army decided it must take the life of one of its own, there was no excuse for the execution being conducted in a way that was less humane than it needed to be. It does only take one bullet to kill a man, so why was there such a variation in the size of the firing squad – even allowing for such things as the exigencies of the service, which in time of conflict was more likely to lead to a smaller rather than a larger firing squad? Whether the condemned man was blindfolded for his benefit or for that of the firing squad is an interesting point of debate, but a simple three-cornered bandage, as specified in the notes given to Guilford, should have been the norm. Why then was at least one man made to wear a back-to-front gas mask, which would surely have increased the horror of his last moments, and would have similarly affected the firing squad and others present?

I felt uncomfortable as I read about military prisoners who had been subjected to Field Punishment No.2 then being used in various capacities during executions, and also recovering wounded men who were deemed unfit to return to active service but fit enough to hold a rifle as a member of a firing squad. Even allowing for the standards of the time, this could never have been an ethical, reasonable or proportionate use of such men.

In the twenty-first century, where military action is constrained by codes of conduct, serious breaches still occur even in an age of twenty-four-hour news coverage and embedded reporters, meaning these rapidly come to the attention of politicians and the public. I would contend that the lack of a regulatory framework for executions in the First World War meant that questionable things could and did happen, but because of the practices of the times they received no publicity. I could not find one example of a news story from the Western Front, or a piece of film, that was published or shown during the years of the First World War concerning executions, almost certainly because of the censorship regime in place and the willingness of the press to conform. If the public and politicians outside of government had known what was happening, even allowing for society's support of the death penalty in civilian life, I believe uproar would have ensued – in a democracy, governments cannot take for granted the support of the population.

Loath as we might be to take criticism from others, some did have more experience of military executions in the First World War than the British. Therefore the observations of a French officer by the name of Massard (Putkowski and Sykes, 1996), who had been present at a number of executions in Vincennes, where some twenty-seven spies and traitors had met their end, would seem to be appropriate and relevant. Massard was present for the executions of Privates Frederick Johnson and Harry McClair of the 2nd Border Regiment on 1 August 1918; they had been sentenced for desertion. Massard's recollections make a number of interesting observations, including that the men were attended by a 'huge padre of alcoholic appearance'.

Massard was horrified by the conduct of the executions, with both men 'tied up from head to toe like sausages', making it impossible for the men to move. As a result, they looked like shop window mannequins as they were conveyed in a flatbed lorry to the execution site. On their arrival, Massard noted with distaste that the army chaplain 'mumbled some words and then went off to eat!' He summed up the execution, conducted by two separate firing squads of six men each, as follows: 'No military complements, no parade, no music, no march past; a hideous death without drums or trumpets.'

It is difficult to read Massard's recollections without feeling a level of bewilderment and anger. These executions took place nine months after Guilford was handed a set of notes setting out the conduct of an execution. The size of the firing squads was different, six men instead of ten, and the condemned men had been bound in such a way that they could not move, while Guilford's notes speak only of having their wrists bound. The behaviour of the army chaplain is also a cause for concern, as he appeared to display a lack of interest in the proceedings and in the condemned men. Who decided that these executions should be conducted in this way? Although at this distance in time we will never know their names, suspicion must surely fall on either the men's commanding officer or the APM, as it is hard to see that it could have been anyone else. My feeling is that it was more likely to have been the APM because the APM was likely to have been more experienced regarding executions, and the regimental officers would have been only too happy to leave arrangements to them.

The death penalty for murder in civilian life was not abolished until the Murder (Abolition of Death Penalty) Act 1965 suspended its use in England, Wales and Scotland (but not in Northern Ireland), and substituted a mandatory sentence of life imprisonment. The Act further provided that if, before the expiry of the five-year suspension, each House of Parliament passed a resolution to make the effect of the Act permanent, then it would finally be abolished. In 1969 the Labour Home Secretary, James Callaghan, proposed a motion to make the

Act permanent, which was carried in the House of Commons on 16 December 1969, and a similar motion was carried in the House of Lords on 18 December 1969. The death penalty for murder was abolished in Northern Ireland on 25 July 1973 under the Northern Ireland (Emergency Provisions) Act 1973. Despite its abolition, there are still many people who would support its restoration.

In the years of the First World War, there was strong support for the death penalty across all elements of society, and so it is no surprise that it not only existed but was enforced in the military. Those serving on the Western Front and the other theatres of the First World War knew the consequences of committing offences under military law, and undoubtedly a number would have supported the use of the death penalty. Many, though, sympathised with the condemned men because they understood what they had been through, as well as their personal circumstances, far better than those who had recommended and confirmed the death sentence. I would contend, however, that despite the standards and practices of the times, the death penalty for those serving in the military and committing offences that had no parallel in civilian life, was both wrong-headed and illogical – and those involved in its administration should have realised that was the case.

Army discipline comes from training, and then more training, backed up by a set of rules enshrined in military law, ignorance of which, as in civilian law, does not form an acceptable defence. The British Army supported the death penalty because it argued that it needed it to maintain discipline and keep an army in the field, but as Lieutenant-Colonel Meyler, who later became MP for Blackpool, said, 'You train your soldiers not to be impressed by fear, to despise fear, and then you go and bring out ... this death sentence which is supposed to improve their discipline by means of fear. The whole thing is illogical.'

Ernest Thurtle also shared Meyler's view when he wrote that the War Office, in the last resort, had defended the death penalty on the grounds of military necessity. He interpreted this as demonstrating that it was only the threat of being shot by men of their own side that kept the British soldier fighting, despite the fact that, as he pointed out, the death penalty had not applied to the Australian soldiers. He concluded with the following words:

> no democracy has the right to shoot any man in cold blood, volunteer or conscript, because he is unable to withstand the horrors of modern war. If war cannot be waged without the death penalty, and we take the penalty away, much the worse for the people who make wars but take good care not to fight in them.

The fact that no Australian soldier was executed in the First World War, despite pressure from Sir Douglas Haig for them to adopt the death penalty, is for me the centrepiece of the case for the illogicality of the British Army's approach to capital offences in the military. I say illogical because there is absolutely no evidence that the performance and discipline of the Australian soldiers was undermined because the Australian military did not have the death penalty as a means of ensuring conformity and control. I find it hard to believe that no Australian soldier ever fell asleep on guard duty or committed the other offences that would have meant a death sentence for their British counterparts, and you would be a brave person to argue that they were less effective as a result.

Support for the death penalty is based on the principles of punishment and deterrence, but in the British Army, with the exception of murder and treason, the capital offences did not have an equivalent in the civilian world. If you are prepared to accept that the British Army in the midst of the First World War needed not only to have, but also to impose, the death sentence, then the assumption would be that the execution would not only punish the individual but also act as a deterrent to others. It is the deterrent aspect that can be the only justification for those public military executions that took place, demonstrating to the men in the battalions and regiments concerned what they could expect if they decided to, for example, desert. From the evidence I have been able to gather it seems that the deterrence aspect was just not apparent in many of the executions, to the point where soldiers simply stopped believing that they happened. In addition, if the death sentence was such a deterrent, then why had some of those who were eventually executed deserted a number of times?

Even allowing for the procedures of the times, the way that decisions leading to the confirmation of a death sentence were made was not just wrong-headed but, in fact, plain wrong. This view is based on the fact that military law was changed in September 1914 to allow for the decision of a field court martial to be enacted quickly; the condemned man's right to an appeal was also taken away.

After the First World War, the British Army and its supporters made much of the fact that only 10 per cent of those sentenced to death were actually executed, but behind that figure there exists a real cause for concern. In civilian life, for example, which after all existed in parallel with military life during the First World War and only a few miles distant from it, if a murder was committed, the perpetrator would be arrested and taken before a court and, if subsequently found guilty, would be sentenced to death by the judge in that court. The law allowed for an appeal process and once that was exhausted the sentence would be carried out. In the British Army, however, things were done somewhat differently: once a soldier had been found guilty of a capital offence, he would not be told the sentence but would have to wait while his case passed up through the decision-making tree. It would appear that confirmation of the sentence depended on the man's senior officers and ultimately the commander-in-chief taking a view as to whether an example needed to be made, based on the perceived discipline and or performance of the individual's battalion or regiment. So once again, even allowing for the practices of the times, this cannot have been right if the sentence was being determined not by the offence itself, but for reasons unconnected to the offence. Was it right that the decision concerning a man's life could hinge on the perceived discipline and performance of those he served with?

The only explanation for the denial of an appeal for those soldiers condemned to death has to be the needs of the exigencies of the service, as perceived by the military hierarchy. If the condemned man had a right of appeal then very few men would have chosen not to exercise it, which would have placed a burden on the system. I suspect also that there was a strong desire to keep matters in-house where they could be contained, because an appeal process could have led to appeals being considered by those from a non-military background who may have questioned the courts martial process, the lack of evidence, the lack of qualified legal representation and the reasons why a sentence had been confirmed.

Once the sentence had been confirmed then the execution would take place within a matter of hours or, in some cases, minutes, giving the individual concerned little time to prepare or, even if they were able, to draw attention to their plight.

In the early years of the twentieth century, Britain was a society with distinct social classes, yet even accepting that was the custom of the time, it is indefensible that class played such a prominent role in the British Army's enforcement of discipline. As was the case with the Australians, it is hard to believe that British Army officers did not commit any capital offences – of course they did, but they were just dealt with differently.

It is hard to understand how it could be the case that only three officers were executed in the First World War, with one of those being for murder. In 1916, Sir Douglas Haig wrote that desertion by an officer should be treated more severely than with the other ranks, but his wish changed nothing. Underperforming officers were taken out of the front line and either sent back to Britain or placed in roles behind the lines. On the rare occasions that an officer was charged and found guilty, they were more likely to be cashiered or demoted. Unlike their men, officers could and did appeal, and many were pardoned and restored to their rank by King George V in the years after the war had ended. Sadly, but unsurprisingly, the opponents of pardons for those executed were not keen to accept this as a reason for pardons to be granted, albeit posthumously, to the other ranks.

There is also evidence that the private soldier was viewed by some officers as virtually worthless. This is not a re-run of the 'lions led by donkeys' debate, but if a condemned man was viewed in that way then it is not a huge leap to a position where he is viewed as expendable. For me, the issue of class is one of the more uncomfortable aspects of the British Army's adherence to the death penalty because, unlike civilian law, it did not apply to all men equally. The case of Private James Crozier is a blatant example of this, as is the part played by Major (later Brigadier) Crozier. Major Crozier was faced with two men who had deserted, one being an officer and the other a young private soldier, and he was dismayed that those above him decided that no further action was to be taken against the officer. However, despite the glaring unfairness involved, he did not hesitate to recommend that Private Crozier should be executed.

Sir Douglas Haig's mantra, 'truth could be abandoned in the cause of the war effort', leads to another area of concern: namely, the lack of transparency on the part of the military hierarchy and the politicians. It was the army's procedure up until 1917 for its Records Office bluntly to inform families that their family member had been sentenced to death and that this sentence had been carried out, resulting in the forfeiture of all rights to campaign medals and benefits, which had the effect of leaving many families destitute. The Army Records Office could only send such letters if it was informed that a sentence had been carried out and yet, up until 1917, some commanding officers included those executed in the lists of men killed in action. This situation ended in 1917, much to the army's dismay, when the government decided in November of that year that the families of those executed were to be informed that their loved ones had died on active service. This had been an informal procedure on the part of some commanding officers, though it is impossible to say with any confidence whether such officers were motivated by concerns for the men's families or a desire, for whatever reason, to keep things quiet, thereby protecting themselves and ultimately the army.

In the early years of the First World War, the government itself was reluctant to admit that executions were taking place, or the numbers involved. It could be argued, therefore, that the government and the military hierarchy's behaviour seemed to be bordering on embarrassment about what was happening. I believe that, certainly up until 1916 when conscription was brought in, one of their concerns would have been the possible impact on recruitment if the facts became known. The government could not afford to take the British people for granted and risk alienating them, which might have been the result if the scale of the executions had become known.

Neither the military hierarchy nor the government did much to dispel the feeling that they had something to hide even when the war ended. Families, politicians and other interested parties were prevented from gaining access to the courts martial papers on the basis that only defendants could request these, and as they had been shot no one else had a right to them. Furthermore, the papers relating to those executed were initially embargoed for 100 years. The army also engaged in 'weeding out' – which today would be referred to as redacting – what it considered to be sensitive documents from battalion and regimental diaries and routine orders, in what it admitted was an attempt to 'thwart the inquisitive'.

One hundred years later it is still possible to find examples where the inquisitive are being thwarted. On Wednesday 9 April 2014, under the headline 'MoD tries to block its own book on Helmand', *The Times* reported that the Ministry of Defence was attempting to block a highly critical study of British and American 'naivety' in the Helmand district of Afghanistan. The author claimed that the 'MoD was more interested in protecting its reputation than learning from a conflict that has cost 448 British lives'. If the words 'learning from a conflict' and '448 British lives' are replaced by 'learning from practice' and '302 British and Commonwealth lives', then it could just as easily be a piece about British Army executions on the Western Front from 1914 to 1918. To progress, there is a need to be reflective, posing questions to gain understanding that can then change future practice – something which those in Whitehall seem reluctant to do, and therefore nothing changes.

In 1919 the army had shown that it was aware of the public mood and the likely consequences for its ability to retain the death penalty, as evidenced in the extract from the Darling Committee Report included in Chapter 8:

> Even during the continuance of hostilities there was very strong feeling both in the country and in the House of Commons against the infliction of the death penalty for military offences. Now that hostilities have ceased it can confidently be stated that the effect on this country of a death penalty might lead to an agitation which might be difficult to control and in all probability would jeopardise the prospects of maintaining the death penalty for military offences in time of peace when the Annual Army (Act) comes before the Houses of Parliament.

Despite this, the army still maintained its support for the death penalty, although it proved to be a losing battle. In stages, from 1928 to 1930 and then finally in 1998, it was eventually abolished. Abolition was not to be the end of matters because there was then the Shot at Dawn campaign that sought pardons for those executed, with the exception of those sentenced for murder or treason. This campaign was opposed by some who could see no purpose, for a variety of reasons, in the granting of general pardons, but their position was somewhat undermined by the fact that officers had been pardoned by King George V, so a precedent had been established. Eventually, in 2006, the campaign achieved its purpose. I believe that those who played a part in the campaign to get those executed pardoned deserve to be recognised, because they took on the establishment and succeeded.

To say that I have enjoyed this research would be wrong, given the subject matter, but I have found it extremely interesting and at times my response to what I have read and discovered has been one of anger, sadness and frustration. In writing this book, I have deliberately chosen to look at matters post-sentence, which means that I have not written about the back stories of those condemned – their offences, their personal circumstances at the time, or the courts martial process – unless some context was required.

I am sure that the majority of people reading this book will have experienced a similar range of feelings by the time they have reached the end. This is not the most glorious chapter in the history of the British Army and the War Office/Ministry of Defence. In terms of transparency and the control of information it seems that the lessons of the past have not been learnt, but at least now the immediacy and variety of news coverage ensures that the public is better informed, despite the best efforts of the generals and the Whitehall 'machine'.

In all probability, my book and its analysis will infuriate some, who, as a result, will argue that, coming from a non-military background, how could I possibly understand the pressures on those army officers who were charged with fighting a war that was unlike any that had gone before. My answer would have to be: of course they are right in terms of my background, but I would make the point that I did not have any preconceived ideas when I started the research for this book and my analysis is based solely on what I have read and discovered. In any event, my book was written to inform a wider audience who, if sufficiently interested, will then engage in some wider reading around the subject and form their own opinion, and maybe answer for themselves some of the questions my research and analysis has posed.

And if research does raise more questions than it answers then let me pose a final, if possibly inconvenient, question. Babington in his statistical breakdown of those executed gave a figure of thirty-one soldiers executed on the Western Front for murder. Those executed for murder were never included in the campaign for pardons because murder was an offence punishable by death in both the military and civilian worlds, which leads to my final question. How certain can we be, given the inadequacies of the courts martial process, that those charged with murder were properly investigated, tried and sentenced?

Finally, I think my research has given me an understanding of why David Lewis feels that there is still unfinished business where British Army executions in the First World War are concerned.

The Old Brown Teapot

by A.R. (David) Lewis

Standing in a Flanders Trench, the young soldier
peered into the gloom, as he waited for stand down,
which would signal the dawn, and rest from duty.
His mind turned to thoughts of home.
Sounds of shells, gunfire, war,
blotted out by warm caressing visions,
of a kitchen, glowing in lamp light.
His mother busy preparing tea.
The Old Brown Teapot, warming on the hob.
His thoughts turned to dreams,
and he fell asleep at his post.
To be awakened by shaking and shouting,
the Sergeant and Officer demanding explanations.
Inevitably the Court Martial followed.
The verdict as expected 'Guilty',
punishment death by firing squad.
They pinned a white patch on his chest,
tied him to a chair, then read out the charge.
He did not hear it, his mind was fixed on the Old Brown
    Teapot.
In the little cottage, the fire had gone out,
his mother paused, shivered as she rekindled the fire.

In the bright flame she saw her son's face,
she picked up the teapot, the face disappeared,
suddenly she knew, the teapot fell from her grasp.
She sank to the floor to pick up the pieces.
For sixteen years she had treasured them both.
Now they were gone, Lost to her forever.

As powerful as that poem is, perhaps the final word should go to a veteran by the name of Harry Littler:

It's worried me all my life. Anyone who has been on a battlefield would know. Sometimes those chaps didn't know where they were, never mind what they were doing. The sight of some of those poor wretches – some of whom had given their all – their nerves shot to pieces, having to face death by firing squad because of a decision by unknown 'red tabs' and branded cowards, in my opinion was an infamy.

Appendix I

STATEMENT MADE BY DR JOHN
REID, ARMED FORCES MINISTER,
ON 24 JULY 1998

First World War (Executions)

With permission, I will make a statement about executions of soldiers and others in the First World War.

I doubt whether anyone who has not gone through the awesome experience of war can ever truly imagine its effects on the emotions of human beings. Some 9 million troops from all sides died during the Great War. Almost 1 million British and Empire soldiers fell, heroes to their nations and a testimony to the awfulness of war.

We rightly remember them still, not only on 11 November, but in ceremonies throughout the year and throughout the globe. Today, I am sure that I am joined by the whole House in once again paying tribute to the courage and fortitude of all who served from throughout Britain and the Empire.

For some of our soldiers and their families, however, there has been neither glory nor remembrance. Just over 300 of them died at the hands not of the enemy, but of firing squads from their own side. They were shot at dawn, stigmatised and condemned – a few as cowards, most as deserters. The nature of those deaths and the circumstances surrounding them have long been a matter of contention. Therefore, last May, I said that we would look again at their cases.

The review has been a long and complicated process, and I have today placed a summary in the Library of the House. I will outline some salient features.

Between 4 August 1914 and 31 March 1920, approximately 20,000 personnel were convicted of military offences under the British Army Act for which the death penalty could have been awarded. That does not include civilian capital offences such as murder. Of those 20,000, something over 3,000 were actually sentenced to death. Approximately 90 per cent of them escaped execution. They had their sentences commuted by their commanders-in-chief.

The remainder, those executed for a military offence, number some 306 cases in all. That is just 1 per cent of those tried for a capital offence, and 10 per cent of those actually sentenced to death. Those 300 or so cases can be examined, because the records were preserved. In virtually all other cases, the records were destroyed. It is the cases of those 300 that many hon. Members, notably my hon. Friend the Member for Thurrock (Mr. Mackinlay), and others outside the House, including the Royal British Legion, have asked us to reconsider with a view to some form of blanket pardon.

Let me make it plain that we cannot and do not condone cowardice, desertion, mutiny or assisting the enemy – then or now. They are all absolutely inimical to the very foundation of our armed forces. Without military discipline, the country could not be defended, and that is never more important than in times of war.

However, the circumstances of the First World War, and the long-standing controversy about the executions, justify particular consideration. We have therefore reviewed every aspect of the cases. We have considered the legal basis for the trials – field general court martial. The review has confirmed that procedures for the court martial were correct, given the law as it stood at the time.

The review also considered medical evidence. Clearly, if those who were executed could be medically examined now, it might be judged that the effects of their trauma meant that some should not have been considered culpable; but we cannot examine them now. We are left with only the records, and in most cases there is no implicit or explicit reference in the records to nervous, or other psychological or medical, disorders. Moreover, while it seems reasonable to assume that medical considerations may have been taken into account in the 90 per cent of cases where sentences were commuted, there is no direct evidence of that, either, as almost all the records of those commuted cases have long since been destroyed.

However frustrating, the passage of time means that the grounds for a blanket legal pardon on the basis of unsafe conviction just do not exist. We have therefore considered the cases individually.

A legal pardon, as envisaged by some, could take one of three forms: a free pardon, a conditional pardon or a statutory pardon. We have given very serious consideration to this matter. However, the three types of pardon have one thing in common – for each individual case, there must be some concrete evidence for overturning the decision of a legally constituted court, which was charged with examining the evidence in those serious offences.

I have personally examined one-third of the records – approximately 100 personal case files. It was a deeply moving experience. Regrettably, many of the records contain little more than the minimum prescribed for this type of court martial – a form recording administrative details and a summary – not a transcript – of the evidence. Sometimes it amounts only to one or two handwritten pages.

I have accepted legal advice that, in the vast majority of cases, there is little to be gleaned from the fragments of the stories that would provide serious grounds for a legal pardon. Eighty years ago, when witnesses were available and the events were fresh in their memories, that might have been a possibility, but the passage of time has rendered it well-nigh impossible in most cases.

So, if we were to pursue the option of formal, legal pardons, the vast majority, if not all, of the cases would be left condemned either by an accident of history which has left us with insufficient evidence to make a judgment, or, even where the evidence is more extensive, by a lack of sufficient evidence to overturn the original verdicts. In short, most would be left condemned, or in some cases re-condemned, 80 years after the event.

I repeat here what I said last May when I announced the review – that we did not wish, by addressing one perceived injustice, to create another. I wish to be fair to all, and, for that reason I do not believe that pursuing possible individual formal legal pardons for a small number, on the basis of impressions from the surviving evidence, will best serve the purpose of justice or the sentiment of Parliament. The point is that now, eighty years after the events and on the basis of the evidence, we cannot distinguish between those who deliberately let down their country and their comrades in arms and those who were not guilty of desertion or cowardice.

Current knowledge of the psychological effects of war, for example, means that we now accept that some injustices may have occurred. Suspicions cannot be completely allayed by examination of the sparse records. We have therefore decided also to reject the option of those who have urged us to leave well alone and to say nothing. To do nothing, in the circumstances, would be neither compassionate nor humane.

Today, there are four things that we can do in this House, which sanctioned and passed the laws under which these men were executed. First, with the knowledge now available to us, we can express our deep sense of regret at the loss of life. There remain only a very few of our fellow countrymen who have any real understanding or memory of life and death in the trenches and on the battlefields of the First World War. This year marks the eightieth anniversary of the end of the war, and we are recalling and remembering the conditions of that war, and all those who endured them, both those who died at the hands of the enemy, and those who were executed. We remember, too, those who did their awful duty in the firing squads.

Secondly, in our regret, and as we approach a new century, let us remember that pardon implies more than legality and legal formality. Pardon involves understanding, forgiveness, tolerance and wisdom. I trust that hon. Members will agree that, while the passage of time has distanced us from the evidence and the possibility of distinguishing guilt from innocence, and has rendered the formality of pardon impossible, it has also cast great doubt on the stigma of condemnation.

If some men were found wanting, it was not because they all lacked courage, backbone or moral fibre. Among those executed were men who had bravely volunteered to serve their country. Many had given good and loyal service. In a sense, those who were executed were as much victims of the war as the soldiers and airmen who were killed in action, or who died of wounds or disease, like the civilians killed by aerial or naval bombardment, or like those who were lost at sea. As the twentieth century draws to a close, they all deserve to have their sacrifice acknowledged afresh. I ask hon. Members to join me in recognising those who were executed for what they were – the victims, with millions of others, of a cataclysmic and ghastly war.

Thirdly, we hope that others outside the House will recognise all that, and that they will consider allowing the missing names to be added to books of remembrance and war memorials throughout the land.

Finally, there is one other thing that we can do as we look forward to a new millennium. The death penalty is still enshrined in our military law for five offences, including misconduct in action and mutiny. I can tell the House that Defence Ministers will invite Parliament to abolish the death penalty for military offences in the British armed forces in peace and in war. [Hon. Members: 'Hear, hear.']

There are deeply held feelings about the executions. Eighty years after those terrible events, we have tried to deal with a sensitive issue as fairly as possible for all those involved. In remembrance of those who died in the war, the poppy fields of Flanders became a symbol for the shattered innocence and the shattered lives of a lost generation. May those who were executed, with the many, many others who were victims of war, finally rest in peace. Let all of us who have inherited the world that followed remember with solemn gratitude the sacrifices of those who served that we might live in peace.

Appendix 2

WRITTEN MINISTERIAL STATEMENT BY DES BROWNE, SECRETARY OF STATE FOR DEFENCE, ON 18 SEPTEMBER 2006

World War I Veterans (Pardons)

The Secretary of State for Defence (Des Browne): On 16 August I announced that the Government plan to seek parliamentary approval for a statutory pardon for service personnel executed for a range of disciplinary offences during the First World War. I am now taking this opportunity to confirm these plans to the House and to provide some further information on our intentions.

I have reviewed carefully the case for granting pardons and concluded that although this is a difficult issue it is right to recognise the exceptional circumstances that gave rise to these executions and to show compassion to the families who have had to live with the associated stigma over the years.

Given the paucity of records for the court martial of those executed, I have taken the view that it would not be appropriate or fair to consider individual pardons under the Royal Prerogative but that a statutory pardon for all members of the group should be introduced. This approach removes the risk of individual cases failing to meet the criteria for a pardon under the Prerogative simply because of lack of evidence.

It is the Government's intention to introduce an amendment to the current Armed Forces Bill during the Lord's Committee Stage to give effect to this. Rather than naming individuals, the amendment will pardon all those executed following conviction by court martial for a range of offences likely to have been strongly influenced by the stresses associated with this terrible war; this will include desertion, cowardice, mutiny and comparable offences committed during the period of hostilities from 4 August 1914 to 11 November 1918. Over 300 individuals from the UK, her dominions and colonies were executed under the 1881 Army Act. We will also seek pardons for those similarly executed under the provisions of the 1911 Indian Army Act, records of whose identities we have not been able to locate. We consider that it would not be appropriate to include in the pardon all capital offences and specifically the offences of murder and treason will be excluded.

In each case, the effect of the pardon will be to recognise that execution was not a fate that the individual deserved but resulted from the particular discipline and penalties considered to be necessary at the time for the successful prosecution of the war. We intend that the amendment should so far as possible remove the particular dishonour that execution brought to the individuals and their families. However, the pardon should not be seen as casting doubt on either the procedures and processes of the time or the judgement of those who took these very difficult decisions.

The pardon would apply to those sentences of execution confirmed and carried out but convictions would not be quashed. The amendment will not create any right to compensation and the Royal Prerogative of Mercy will remain unaffected.

As the amendment would affect the cases of personnel who were serving in the armed forces of a number of dominions and colonies, we are consulting with the Governments of those states or their successors on our plans. We are expecting to receive their responses shortly but I can confirm that our decision has already been welcomed by one of those principally affected. I anticipate the Government's proposal will also be warmly welcomed by the public at large and particularly by the families concerned.

(Taken from Hansard)

Appendix 3

REPORT OF AN ADJOURNMENT DEBATE HELD IN THE HOUSE OF COMMONS ON 3 MARCH 2009: THE STORY OF PRIVATE JAMES SMITH

Motion made, and Question proposed, That this House do now adjourn. – *(Mr McAvoy)*

8.44 pm

Dr Brian Iddon (Bolton South-East) (Lab): Many tragic stories have emerged from the two world wars of 1914 to 1918 and 1939 to 1945. Unbelievable numbers from the British Commonwealth and other men and women from across the world were lost in these conflicts. In my opinion, they were all people of great courage who were willing to put their lives on the line for this country and for freedom from tyranny.

This is the tragic story of James Smith – Jimmy to his friends – who was born in 1891 at 77 Noble Street, which today is in my constituency, and whose mother, Elizabeth, died just after he was born. He was brought up by his devoted maternal aunt, Eliza, and his uncle John in Great Lever in my constituency. Relatives John – known as Jack – and Freda Hargreaves live in Great Lever today. Jack's mother was Jimmy Smith's cousin. Jimmy's story was brought to me by Charles Sandbach and Bill Miles, who are interested in military history and who are campaigning to have Jimmy Smith's name added to the Bolton roll of honour, which is kept in the ceremonial entrance to Bolton town hall.

Mr Jim Devine (Livingston) (Lab): As my hon. Friend knows, the same individuals have been involved in getting the name of someone from my constituency on a roll in that hall. He was 27 years old, and died in 1917, and it was not until the work that these people did in identifying where he came from and his family background that that soldier's name was proudly put on the war memorial.

Dr Iddon: I am grateful for that intervention; it is a story that has been told to me. Indeed, these two gentleman who are interested in military history made a one-hour film about a soldier – not unlike the one I am talking about this evening – who went through the tragedies of World War One. It is a brilliant film that ought to have a wider showing than it has hitherto.

We want Jimmy to be remembered, along with his comrades, every year on Remembrance Day. Jimmy was Charles Sandbach's paternal grandmother's uncle and Charles initially sought the help of my friend Councillor Frank White, former Member of Parliament for Bury and Radcliffe, who is currently president of the Bolton United Veterans' Association, formed in 1906 before the British Legion was established, the second of many such associations to be formed that still exist today.

Private James Smith was the subject of a play, *Early One Morning*, written by Bolton playwright Les Smith and presented at the Octagon theatre in Bolton, with its first performance on 22 October 1998 to mark the eightieth anniversary of the armistice. James Smith initially enlisted in the 1st Battalion Lancashire Fusiliers in 1910, just before his nineteenth birthday, to escape the grinding poverty in which he lived at that time. Although he hardly knew his father James William Smith, who remarried, Jimmy enlisted using his father's address in Noble Street.

2022 Private James Smith trained in Egypt, then served in Karachi, India, before being recalled when World War One was declared. Among his many horrific experiences of that war was the Lancashire landing on W beach at Gallipoli on the morning of 25 April 1915, when his battalion stormed a cliff bristling with Turkish machine guns. No fewer than six of his comrades won Victoria Crosses before breakfast – still an all-time record for such awards. In scaling and taking that cliff, half the battalion were lost on that day.

After enduring the rest of that nightmare campaign, Private James Smith was evacuated in 1916 to France, where he joined volunteers in the 15th Battalion Lancashire Fusiliers, known as the Salford pals. With one good conduct badge at that time, he was soon in the thick of the action again and gained a second good conduct badge. Such were the losses on the Somme that infantrymen were regularly transferred from one regiment to another, and Jimmy was transferred to the 17th Battalion King's Liverpool Regiment, known as the 1st Liverpool pals, on 26 June 1917, with the rank of lance-corporal. He almost lost his life in France on the Somme when, on 11 October 1916, a massive German artillery shell buried him alive on the Transloy ridge, with bits of his friends around him, and shrapnel created a large deep wound on his right shoulder. According to his sister, it was big enough to put a fist in. Fortunately, he was rescued and taken home to Townleys Hospital in Bolton, but in a very poor mental and physical state from which he never recovered. The shocks and horrors of the battles that he had seen had damaged him to such an extent that he was clearly unfit for further service. Those who served with him were well aware of his condition. Today, we would recognise that Jimmy Smith was suffering from serious post-traumatic stress disorder. No such condition was recognised in the Great War, and it was believed that soldiers could recover from shell shock of that kind.

Just 10 days after he returned to the front line, and clearly under a great deal of stress, Jimmy Smith volunteered to give up his stripe and became 52929 Private James Smith. Six days later, he left his post without orders. On 29 December 1916, Jimmy found himself before a field general court martial for a breach of military discipline. He was ordered to do ninety days' field punishment number one and lost one of his good conduct badges. On 15 July 1917, just before the battle of Passchendaele in the Ypres salient, he found himself before a field general court martial for a second time for going absent without leave. He was only 26 years old.

We believe that the court recognised that Private James Smith was in no condition to fight. It spared him a death sentence on that second occasion and ordered him again to do ninety days' field punishment number one, and he lost his second good conduct badge. Unfortunately, the Army never allowed Jimmy to complete that sentence, because the 17th Battalion King's Liverpool Regiment found itself at the Pilckem Ridge, north of the famous town of Ypres. By that time, Jimmy Smith was so unwell that he could not function properly at the front, and his comrades knew it. They tried to ensure that he was given light duties, possibly out of the trenches, but to no avail.

On 30 July 1917, on the eve of the battle of Pilckem Ridge, Jimmy had a breakdown and deserted his post without orders again. At 11 pm, he was seen five miles from the front, wandering about in the town of Poperinghe, where he was arrested. A doctor at a dressing station declared him fit for duty, and Jimmy was charged with desertion. While detained in the military cells at Poperinghe Town Hall, Jimmy was ordered to undertake a two-hour drill. He refused to march and was also charged with disobedience. That was the beginning of the end of Private James Smith. The plain fact is that at that time he should have not been in action but serving his third punishment.

On 22 August 1917, Jimmy found himself before a field general court martial for the third time in seven months. Major Watson, Lieutenant Pierce and Lieutenant Collins came to a unanimous verdict of guilty on both charges. At his trial, he was unrepresented, no defence witnesses were called and he never spoke a word. Jimmy accepted his fate without fear as he was sentenced to death. The court was well aware of his medical history and could have decided to transfer him to the Labour Corps, but no; instead, it decided to make an example of an experienced regular soldier, clearly suffering from serious shell shock having experienced horrors in several battles. The brigadier confirmed sentence on 22 August, the divisional commander on 28 August and the commander-in-chief Field Marshal Haig on 2 September.

Early on the morning of 5 September, a small patrol of soldiers from Jimmy's own unit entered a barn at Kemmel Château in Belgium to clean their weapons prior to re-engagement with the enemy. They were told that, first, they had a special duty to perform, and they were taken outside into a courtyard where they found their friend, Jimmy Smith, blindfolded and tied to an execution chair in front of a wall, with a white target pinned to his tunic, just above his heart. Protesting furiously to the commanding officer, the twelve-man firing squad – eleven privates and a non-commissioned officer – was summarily ordered to execute Jimmy. The lads aimed and fired, the majority deliberately missing the target. However, Jimmy was wounded, the chair was knocked over and he lay writhing in agony on the ground.

The young officer in charge of the firing squad was shaking like a leaf, but he knew now that he had to finish Jimmy off by putting a bullet through his brain with his Webley pistol. He lost his nerve, however, and could not fire the pistol in his hand as Jimmy continued to writhe in agony on the ground.

One of Jimmy's friends, 23643 Private Richard Blundell, who hailed from Everton in Liverpool, was then ordered by the commanding officer to take the Webley pistol and kill Jimmy. Jimmy's death was recorded on that day at 5.51 am. The twelve members of the firing squad were given ten days' leave after that tragic event in the heat of battle. That was unusual.

Richard Blundell died in Liverpool seventy years later in February 1989, when he was well into his nineties. As he fell in and out of consciousness, his son William heard him utter the words, 'What a way to get leave.' Eventually the story that I have just told about Jimmy's execution emerged, and Richard Blundell's final request to his son was to seek forgiveness from Jimmy Smith's family for what he had done. His action on that morning in September 1917 had clearly been on his mind for seventy years. It was the first time that his family can recall his speaking of his experiences in the Great

War. The author of a book on the Liverpool pals had tried unsuccessfully to interview him about his experiences. In my view, Dickie Blundell also faced a life sentence, perhaps worse than the fate of Private James Smith – we will never know.

For a long time after the great war of 1914–18, shame hung over the families of soldiers such as Private James Smith and their names were not added to those of their comrades on our war memorials or rolls of honour, or written into our books of remembrance. However, Mrs Freda Hargreaves has told me that her family felt no shame and that they proudly owned a photograph of Jimmy, which stood over the mantelpiece for many years after the war ended.

After a long campaign, the Labour Government pardoned those soldiers who were shot at dawn, like Private James Smith in 1917. An amendment to the Armed Forces Bill was introduced in the autumn of 2006 to pardon 306 soldiers, and the measure received Royal Assent on 8 November 2006. I am pleased that several colleagues who played an important role in bringing that about are present in the Chamber, and I thank them for being here.

However, Private James Smith's name has still not been added to the book of remembrance in Bolton Town Hall, and I hope that my hon. Friend the Under-Secretary believes that it now should be. I believe that Jimmy Smith was the only soldier from Bolton to be shot at dawn in the Great War. At least today we have recognised him for what he obviously was – by no means a coward, but an extremely brave soldier who was made seriously ill by his traumatic experiences in several battles in the Great War. He is buried in the military cemetery at Kemmel Château in Belgium in grave M.25. On the grave are the words, 'Gone but not forgotten'. I hope that he will always be remembered by the people of Bolton and that his bravery will finally be recognised. In a different way, he also paid the ultimate price for the rest of us. He, too, laid down his life for our freedom, albeit in a different way.

As a footnote, I can tell my hon. Friend that tomorrow evening I expect that Bolton council will agree to add Private

James Smith's name to the roll of honour, and that a ceremony will be held later this year. We have suggested that an appropriate date would be 27 June, which is Armed Services Day.

Bolton council has let it be known that it is prepared to add any other names to its roll of honour that have been missing to date for any reason. I hope that my hon. Friend agrees that all local authorities should be encouraged to follow suit.

8.58 pm

John Reid (Airdrie and Shotts) (Lab): I was not aware of the subject of the debate until about twenty minutes ago. I heard the opening words of my hon. Friend the Member for Bolton South-East (Dr. Iddon) as I left the Chamber, and came back precisely to identify myself with his comments.

I was the Minister who reopened the subject in 1997–98, and I remember it well. In all my years in Government and in the nine posts that I held, I cannot think of any more heart-wrenching task that I took on or was given to me. I personally examined about half the 306 cases, and I am eternally grateful to the officials who went through them, including my military adviser at the time, Simon Gillespie, who sat up, night after night, going through individual cases.

I will not rehearse some of the heart-breaking stories, but I will say this. First, recognising the suffering undergone by those who were executed at dawn and their families is in no way to minimise the equal sacrifices of those who went over the top. I believe that they were all victims. Secondly – this is the only respect in which I differ slightly from my hon. Friend – we should not issue a carte blanche condemnation of the military hierarchy. The truth is that there were some 30,000 cases that could have qualified for a death sentence, but 90 per cent of those concerned did not receive one. Of the 3,000 who did, 90 per cent of those sentences were commuted by the military hierarchy. The records were destroyed, I think in 1924. However, it is extremely likely that the reason why those 2,700 sentences were commuted and only 306 individuals were condemned to death – that is a large number, however, because it is 306 tragedies – is, I believe, although

I cannot prove this because the evidence has gone, probably that in many cases the medical and the mental condition of the person who had been sentenced to death was recognised.

Dr. Iddon: If I gave the impression that I was being critical of the military at that time, it is the wrong impression. They were different times and they were difficult times. People were in the heat of battle and I recognise that they did what they had to do.

John Reid: Perhaps I phrased my comment wrongly. It was not meant as a vicarious criticism of my hon. Friend; it was about whether people recognised shell shock or post-traumatic stress, or whatever it was at the time. I believe that many people did, albeit not because of medical evidence, but because of their personal experience. I think that that is why 2,700 death sentences out of those 3,000 cases were eventually commuted.

Having said those two things, I do not think that there is any doubt that each case was a tragedy. I said earlier that I would not mention any of them, but two stick in my mind. The first involved a young boy in his teens whose last words were: 'Don't tell my mother.' Facing an execution squad, he could think only of the effect that it would have, not on him, when the bullets landed, but on his mother, when the word reached home. The second case was this. At the back of one of the files that I went through, I found, as latterly I found in my father's file – he fought in the Second World War – a little bit for the soldier's will. Soldiers could leave all their worldly possessions in their wills. I recall that the total possessions of one of the soldiers who was executed were the three days' wages that he was owed up to the day of his execution, which he left to his fiancée in Northern Ireland. Such cases deeply moved me.

I was told on the highest legal advice at the time – I can say that now that I am not a Minister – that I could not give a legal pardon. As it was explained to me, I understand that it is impossible to give such a pardon, first, because there were no surviving witnesses, and secondly, because there was no real evidence to overturn a duly arrived at verdict. Thirdly, of those 306 people, even if there had been sufficient evidence in the numerous pages of brown foolscap paper – often they were not transcripts, but summary records of what had happened in the field general court martial – we would have had to test perhaps fourteen cases and left those in the remaining 280 to 290 cases re-condemned. I took the decision at the time that we could not give a legal pardon, but that we should go as far as we could. I will return to that in a second.

I was very grateful to get a second chance at the Ministry of Defence some years later, when I returned as Secretary of State for Defence. During the interval between being Armed Forces Minister and being Secretary of State, I discovered that New Zealand had apparently managed to accomplish that which I had been told was impossible in Britain. Naturally, and in my normal delicate fashion, I interviewed some of my officials who were still there about why that which we had found impossible had been found possible elsewhere. We re-opened the inquiry, and I am glad to say that my successor, my right hon. Friend the Member for Kilmarnock and Loudoun (Des Browne), did a great deal of work on the matter as Defence Secretary. The result is as is known.

The reason that I am supporting my hon. Friend the Member for Bolton South-East tonight is that even at the first stage, in 1998, when we were saying that there was no legal pardon available – I know that my hon. Friend the Member for Thurrock (Andrew Mackinlay) was deeply disappointed by that – I said that, although I found it impossible to give a legal pardon, we would redefine 'pardon' as something other than a legality, and say that, in the eyes of all humanity in this country, those people who had suffered such a terrible fate would indeed be pardoned, in substance if not in legality. Subsequently, of course, we were able to add a legal pardon to that.

At that time, I did three things simultaneously. The first was to say that, as those people had been pardoned, their names should be added back into the books, and on to the memorials and cenotaphs. Secondly, I said that they should be recognised as victims of the Great War, just as everyone else who had fallen in that war was recognised. In that way, their relatives would have a cloud lifted from them. Thirdly – although it was hardly noticed at the time – I announced the abolition of the death penalty in the British armed forces, which was enacted by the next Armed Forces Bill. Yet, some ten years later, some of those names have apparently not been added back in that way.

I hope that what my hon. Friend said tonight was true, and that the case of Jimmy Smith is about to be rectified by having his name added back on to the memorials. I hope, moreover, that that will be an example for other councils and authorities throughout the country, and that they will now recognise what has been recognised over two stages in Parliament, over ten years – namely, that the names should be added back and that the families involved should have no shame.

Having been a Minister, I now have this rare opportunity to say thank you to those who pricked the conscience of Ministers and cajoled, persuaded, drove and whipped them into line. That includes several Members who are here tonight. There cannot be many more worthwhile causes to which they could have applied their minds throughout that period, and I am delighted to be here tonight, no longer as a Minister, but as someone who is part of a group who fully support what my hon. Friend is asking for.

9.07 pm

Andrew Mackinlay (Thurrock) (Lab): I congratulate my hon. Friend the Member for Bolton South-East (Dr. Iddon) on his debate. I mean it from the bottom of my heart when I say that he has written a page in Bolton's history tonight. One thing that emerged from the campaign to grant pardons, which lasted fourteen years in this place, was the fact that this part of British history had been suppressed, and not explained. I believe that history has to be written with clarity and precision, and that includes the parts with which the establishment are unhappy and uncomfortable.

One of the delights of getting the pardons in 2006 was the fact that so many of our countrymen and women – and school students in particular – had learned more about the First World War as a result of the campaign. Through my hon.

Friend, I want to congratulate Bolton council on its initiative. I have visited the town hall at Poperinghe, where this soldier's first trial took place, on many occasions, and I have seen a post of execution there. Many people were executed in Poperinghe town hall's courtyard. I have also been to Kemmel. I hope that those on Bolton council, and many of the schools there, will take that short trip across to Belgium, so that people can reflect on this soldier and the many others from the Bolton area who lie buried in sacred territory there.

Dr Iddon: I have a great deal of respect for my hon. Friend, especially regarding the campaign we are discussing tonight. He might like to know that I intend to send this speech to the secondary schools in my constituency, so that they are made aware of a little part of their history.

Andrew Mackinlay: I think that that is a wonderful initiative, and I know that other Members of Parliament will want to follow suit in according respect to soldiers with roots in their constituency.

The Minister of State and his predecessor went to great lengths to mark the ninetieth anniversary of the Armistice – and they did so very successfully, as three veterans were in attendance. That means that this is not ancient history: those people, living beings from the great conflict, were actually there. My follow-up point – my hon. Friend's contribution this evening endorses it – is that just as the American Civil War has become a part of the American psyche, so has the First World War become part of ours. The conflict in which the soldier we have commemorated tonight took part represents a seminal moment in our history. When this soldier went to war, there were cavalry participating and many of the combating forces wore bright uniforms; yet by the end of the war, we had seen weapons of mass destruction and bombers. At the same time, there was tremendous social change with the extension of women's suffrage and greater popular representation in this place after the war.

We cannot, therefore, overdo this issue. My hon. Friend has reinforced the importance of the First World War tonight – it is something we need to understand and we need to reflect more on the brave soldiers who fought just like the soldier from Bolton – so I would encourage the Minister to do more to widen access to information about World War One and to encourage school students to study it, to reflect on it and to commemorate the brave struggle of men who did their very best on behalf of their country in this most awful conflict, which still has its resonance today.

9.12 pm

The Parliamentary Under-Secretary of State for Defence (Mr Kevan Jones): I congratulate my hon. Friend the Member for Bolton South-East (Dr. Iddon) on securing tonight's debate to highlight the tragic story of Private James Smith and on his campaign to press for the local authorities in Bolton to add this soldier's name to their book of remembrance. I also thank my Right hon. Friend the Member for Airdrie and Shotts (John Reid) for his contribution and I pay tribute to his involvement in the process of finally getting pardons for these individuals. I pay tribute also to my hon. Friend the Member for Thurrock (Andrew Mackinlay) for his tenacious campaign to secure the pardons. I know that he worked closely with an old constituent of mine from when I was a member of Newcastle city council – John Hipkin from Walkergate in Newcastle, who wrote a book and was unrelenting in his campaign to secure the pardons.

In 1998, on the eightieth anniversary of the Armistice, the poet laureate, Andrew Motion, wrote: 'Those guns may have fallen silent eighty years ago, but their echoes neither die nor even fade away.'

I reflected on those words when, on the ninetieth anniversary last November, we witnessed a very moving ceremony at the Cenotaph at which the three surviving UK-resident veterans of World War One laid wreaths to commemorate those who lost their lives in that great war. Sadly, one of them has passed away since that commemoration.

There are few alive today who have personal memories of those who marched away to war, but never came back.

However, across the UK, millions of men, women and – as my hon. Friend the Member for Thurrock said – children shared that poignant moment through the medium of television, and nowadays through the internet. I reinforce his point about ensuring that these tragic events are not forgotten and that future generations learn from them.

Clearly, the First World War is part of the UK's culture, which is not surprising. It represented war on an industrial scale, and I do not think that any family in any community throughout the United Kingdom was untouched. My office in the Sacriston Community Centre contains a list of names of the fallen in the small mining village of Sacriston. Anyone who looks at the list and notes the number of individuals who fell in that small community will appreciate that it must have had a devastating impact, which I do not think we can imagine in modern times.

We must not forget the events of that time. My hon. Friend the Member for Bolton South-East has done two things tonight. Obviously he has raised a very important case, but, as the hon. Member for Thurrock said, he has not only put on record his tribute to this individual but raised a wider issue, and I thank him for that.

A part of my job that I find fascinating is the history of my Department, and the living history with which we are dealing today.

Mr Devine: Speaking of living history, a constituent of mine, John Patterson, flew on thirty-seven bombing missions in the Second World War and ended the war flying around Africa with Lord Mountbatten. He now visits schools to explain exactly what things were like during the war: real live history. I do not know whether we have a checklist of such people who are still alive and can tell real stories, right up to this moment, including people who are serving in Afghanistan and Iraq. As a local Member of Parliament, I have no way of contacting those people. A checklist would preserve the memory of people who have been in combat, and allow some contact with those who are currently in combat.

Madam Deputy Speaker (Sylvia Heal): Order. I have no desire to take anything away from the valued work that those individuals have done, but I think the hon. Gentleman will have noted the title of tonight's Adjournment debate. Perhaps he will be able to raise his point with the Minister on another occasion.

Mr Jones: I will of course follow your guidance, Madam Deputy Speaker, but my hon. Friend has raised an interesting point. My hon. Friend the Member for Bolton South-East said that he would send copies of the report of tonight's debate to schools, with the aim of communicating the facts to future generations, and my hon. Friend the Member for Livingston (Mr Devine) has spoken of veterans visiting schools to pass on their memories.

In Fromelles in northern France, the graves of 400 British and Australian soldiers were recently discovered. A project is now under way, involving the Australian Government and the Commonwealth War Graves Commission, to recover, identify where possible and rebury those remains in the first newly created CWGC (Commonwealth War Graves Commission) cemetery since the Second World War. That has stimulated a great deal of interest, not just in this country but, according to my Australian counterparts, in Australia as well.

Increased participation not just in the educational projects that have been mentioned tonight but in genealogy means that many relatives are researching their family histories and uncovering facts surrounding their forebears for the first time. Some of those discoveries have been disturbing, revealing executions during the First World War.

As my hon. Friend the Member for Bolton South-East pointed out, some of the relatives knew the circumstances of their loved ones' deaths, and certainly did not see them as a cause for shame or any stain on the character of their families. However, I hope that the granting of the statutory pardon in November 2006 has ensured that relatives who did feel shame have experienced some relief, and have recognised that no shame attaches to any of the individuals who were executed or their families. The stigma of dishonour should have been well and truly lifted.

Those executions were tragic episodes, but as the hon. Member for Thurrock pointed out, they must be set against the unprecedented scale of the slaughter during the First World War. Granting the pardon may have little meaning for the individual men, but to the individual families it has meant a great deal.

Thankfully, public perception has changed. That is why, when we introduced the pardon in 2006, it was broadly welcomed by most individuals, although I recognise the strong disagreements that there have been about the issue over many years.

As my hon. Friend the Member for Bolton South-East has said, Private Smith is officially commemorated by his headstone in Kemmel Chateau military cemetery. His name also appears on the Commonwealth War Graves Commission 'Debt of Honour' register. Additionally, symbolic wooden stakes are set around the 'Shot at Dawn' memorial at the National Memorial Arboretum near Lichfield, Staffordshire. Those bear the names of British or Commonwealth servicemen executed during the First World War. I was privileged in January to visit that memorial. I recommend that hon. Members who have not had a chance visit the National Memorial Arboretum. The 'Shot at Dawn' memorial is a simple but moving memorial. Private Smith is among those individuals who are commemorated there.

The Cenotaph, the nation's war memorial, bears only the inscription 'The Glorious Dead' and the dates of the two world wars. No distinction is made in respect of race, gender, colour, creed, or place or circumstances of death of those whom it commemorates. So, too, in the thousands of cemeteries and memorials across the world, without distinction, the Commonwealth War Graves Commission officially commemorates all the men and women who died in the service of Britain and her empire during the First World War. Many do not appreciate that, from the outset, those who were executed by firing squad were commemorated equally with their comrades who died in other circumstances during the First World War. The commission provided identical graves and appropriate headstones for their graves. Some of those graves were lost later.

While commending any initiative that commemorates the sacrifices of those who served in Her Majesty's armed forces, it is important to understand that, beyond the official commemoration to mark a serviceman's final resting place, the Government do not have responsibility for either the funding or maintenance of many memorials such as the one at Bolton town hall. As my hon. Friend and many hon. Members know, there are around 70,000 war memorials in the United Kingdom and they take a wide variety of forms, including books, to which my hon. Friend referred, windows, lichgates, playing fields and buildings – even hospitals, chapels and community halls.

I know that the names of many of those executed men have already been added to many local war memorials as a result of local pressure or family initiatives. I think that that is appropriate; those individuals should be added to those local memorials. I fully support the inclusion of Private Smith's name in his local book of remembrance and I am very pleased to hear that Bolton council will agree tomorrow to add Private James Smith's name to that roll of honour. It is a fitting tribute that his name will be added to the roll of honour. My hon. Friend has paid him a great tribute tonight by speaking about him many years after his death and by putting him on the record of the House, so that future generations can not only read the debate but ensure that we do not forget about brave individuals such as Private Smith.

Question put and agreed to.

9.24 pm

House adjourned.

Appendix 4

THE LAST LETTER HOME FROM PRIVATE ALBERT TROUGHTON OF THE 1ST ROYAL WELCH FUSILIERS, WHO WAS EXECUTED ON 22 APRIL 1915, HAVING BEEN FOUND GUILTY OF DESERTION

(Reproduced by kind permission of Mr Joe O'Loughlin: www.joeoloughlin.co.uk)

Dear Mother, and Father, Sisters and Brothers,

Just a few lines to let you know I am in the best of health and hope you are mother. I am sorry to have to tell you that I am to be shot tomorrow at 7 o'clock in the morning the 22nd April. I hope you will take it in good part and not upset yourself. I shall die like a soldier, so goodbye mother, father, sisters and brothers, if any left. Remember me to Mr. Kendell and them who knew me. Mother I am very sorry nothing happened to me at Ypres, I should not have went away and then I might have stood a good chance of being still alive, but I think that they are paying the debt at the full rate. I thought the most they would give me would be about ten years. It is worse than waiting to be hung.

I hope you got my letters; which I sent you while waiting for my court martial. It seems that something told me I would be shot, so I think the time has come for me to die ... I am only a common soldier and all civilians should know that I have fought for my country in hail, sleet and snow. To the trenches we have to go. All my comrades have been slaughtered which I think everyone should know. When our regiment was captured, the Colonel loudly strained 'Everyone for hiself', but on and on I fought and got clear of the German trenches. This is the punishment I get for getting clear of the Germans … I have wrote my last letter to you all at home, so mother don't be angry with me because I have gone to rest, and pray for me, and I will pray for you. Remember me to Mr. Newbold and tell him about it … I have been silly to go away but if you knew how worried I was, and almost off my head. Think how we had been slaughtered at the beginning of the war … You think they would have a bit of pity for those who are living for their country. Goodbye to all at home. Goodbye, Goodbye.

From your Son,
Albert.

BIBLIOGRAPHY

Allen, P., *Shot at Dawn: The Life and Death of Private James Crampton*, Scarborough Maritime Heritage Website (www. scarboroughsmaritimeheritage.org.uk/scarboroughsocial-history/greatwarshotatdawn.php).

Allison, W. and Fairley, J. (1986), *The Monocled Mutineer*, Quartet Books, London.

Arthur, M. (2002), *Forgotten Voices of the Great War: A New History of WW1 in the Words of the Men and Women Who Were There*, Ebury Press, London.

Babington, A. (2002), *For the Sake of Example: Capital Courts-Martial, 1914–1920*, Penguin, London

Banning, S.T. (1923), *Military Law Made Easy*, reprinted by Amazon, Marston Gate, Milton Keynes.

Baxter, A. (2014), *We Will Not Cease*, Cape Catley, Auckland.

Bickersteth, E. (1996), *Bickersteth Diaries, 1914–18*, Pen & Sword Books Ltd, Barnsley.

Blackburne, H. (1932), *This Also Happened on the Western Front*, Hodder & Stoughton, London.

Brown, M. (1999), *Tommy Goes to War*, Tempus Publishing Ltd, Stroud.

Brown, M. (2001), *The Western Front*, Pan Macmillan, London.

Corns, C. and Hughes-Wilson, J. (2001), *Blindfold and Alone*, Cassell, London.

Corrigan, G. (2004), *Mud, Blood and Poppycock*, Cassell, London.

Crozier, F.P. (1930), *A Brass Hat in No Man's Land*, Naval and Military Press, Uckfield, Sussex.

Crozier, F.P. (1937), *The Men I Killed*, Michael Joseph, London.

Cullen, K. (12 November 2000), 'A Remembrance for Those Who Fled', *Boston Sunday Globe*.

David, S. (2013), *100 Days to Victory: How the Great War was Fought and Won*, Hodder and Stoughton Ltd, London.

Department of Foreign Affairs, 'Shot at Dawn report into the Courts Martial and Execution of Twenty Six Irish Soldiers by the British Army during World War 1', October 2004, available at www.shotatdawncampaignirl.com/ShotatDawnIrishGovernmentConfidentialReportOct2004.pdf (accessed 21 January 2015).

Dunn, J.C. (1989), *The War the Infantry Knew 1914–1919*, Cardinal, London.

Fiennes, P. (2012), *To War with God*, Mainstream Publishing, Edinburgh and London.

Graham, S. (2009), *A Private in the Guards*, Bibliographical Centre for Research, Colorado, USA.

Hastings, M. (2013), *Catastrophe, Europe Goes to War 1914*, HarperCollins, London.

Holden, W. (1998), *Shell Shock: The Psychological Impact Of War*, Channel 4 Books, London.

Holmes, R. (2005), *Tommy: The British Soldier on the Western Front 1914–1918*, Harper Perennial, London.

Jones, S. (16 August 2006), 'Shot at Dawn: The Soldiers' Stories', *Guardian*.

Kennedy, P.J., 'An Eye-Witness Account', The National Archives, reference WO 95/1617.

Lewis-Stempel, J. (2011), *Six Weeks: The Short and Gallant Life of the British Officer in the First World War*, Orion, London.

Linklater, J. (25 July 1998), 'The Boy Who Lied to Fight but was then Shot at Dawn', *Herald Scotland*.

Linklater, J. (accessed 19 March 2014), 'Saving Private Byers', www.aftermathww1.co.uk.

Lister, D. (2013), *Die Hard, Aby!*, Pen & Sword Books Ltd, Barnsley.

Macdonald, L. (1991), *1914–1918: Voices and Images of the Great War*, Penguin, London.

Marr, A. (2009), *The Making of Modern Britain: From Queen Victoria to VE Day*, Pan Macmillan, London.

Moore, W. (1999), *The Thin Yellow Line*, Wordsworth, London.

Moran, J. (2013), *Anatomy of Courage*, Constable, London.

Paxman, J. (2013), *Great Britain's Great War*, Penguin, London.

Plowman, M. (2001), *A Subaltern on the Somme*, Naval and Military Press, Uckfield, East Sussex.

Putkowski, J. and Sykes, J. (1998), *Shot at Dawn: Executions in World War One by Authority of the British Army Act*, Pen & Sword Books Ltd, Barnsley.

Putkowski, J. and Dunning, M. (2012), *Murderous Tommies*, Pen and Sword Military, Barnsley.

Scott, F.G. (2009), *The Great War as I Saw It*, Naval and Military Press, Uckfield, East Sussex.

Sheffield, G. (2012), *The Chief: Douglas Haig and the British Army*, Aurum Press Ltd, London.

Sheffield, G. and Bourne, J. (eds) (2005), *Douglas Haig: War Diaries and Letters 1914–1918*, Weidenfeld and Nicholson, London.

Snape, M. (2004), 'British Army Chaplains and Capital Courts-Martial in the First World War', in K. Cooper and J. Gregory (eds), 'Retribution, Repentance, and Reconciliation', *Studies in Church History*, 40, 2004, pp. 357–68.

Stormont-Gibbs, C.C. (1992), *From the Somme to the Armistice: The Memoirs of Captain Stormont-Gibbs*, Gliddon Books, Norwich.

Steuart, R.H.J. (1931), *March Kind Comrade*, Sheed and Ward, London.

Suffield, S. (winter 1987), 'One Man's War, Stand To', *Journal of the Western Front Association*, no. 21.

Sweeney, J. (14 November 1999), 'Lest We Forget the 306 "Cowards" We Executed', *Observer*.

Taylor-Whiffen, P. (2003), 'Shot at Dawn: Cowards, Traitors or Victims?' wrvsmorayheritagememories.wordpress.com/useful-links/bbc-scottish-history-page/world-war-two-websites/bbc-world-war-one-history.

Thurtle, E. (2013), *Shootings at Dawn: The Army Death Penalty at Work*, Hard Press Publishing, Miami.

Tucker, J.F. (1978), *Johnny Get Your Gun: Personal Narrative of the Somme, Ypres and Arras*, Harper Collins, London.

Van Emden, R. (2002), *The Trench: Experiencing Life on the Front Line, 1916*, Transworld Publishers, London.

Van Emden, R. (2012), *The Quick and the Dead*, Bloomsbury Paperbacks, London.

Warren, T. (2009), Campaign for Soldiers Shot at Dawn, BBC News (http://news.bbc.co.uk/1/hi/england/8117237.stm).

Williams, M. (2013), *With Innocence and Hope*, You Caxton Publication, London.

Williamson, B.J. (2005), *Happy Days in France*, Naval and Military Press, Uckfield, East Sussex.

Winter, D. (1979), *Death's Men: Soldiers of the Great War*, Penguin, London.

Imperial War Museum

Andrews, M., sound archive, 4770/1.

Esler, Captain M.S., diary, catalogue no. 407.

Gameson, L., private papers, catalogue no. 612.

Mortimer, J.G., diary, 75/21/1.

Rogers, Reverend T.C., letters, Misc 77/107/1.

Walkinton, Captain M.L., diary, DS/MISC/41

INDEX

Adamson, Private James 103
Agabeg, Second Lieutenant
    I.W.F. 79
Alexander, CQMS William
    88–90
Andrews, Martin 87
Anley, Brigadier-General
    F.G. 138
Annandale, Lieutenant
    Arthur 64
Ansted, Private Alfred 87
Army Act 11, 21, 27–8, 30, 32,
    34, 43, 127, 133, 142, 160,
    173, 180
Ashdown, Lord Paddy 145
Atkinson, L/Cpl Alfred 49

Babbington, Judge Anthony
    60, 68, 129, 136, 170
Bateman, Private Joseph 34,
    90, 97

Baxter, Archie 31
Beverstein, Private Abraham
    55, 65–7, 72–3
Bickersteth, Reverend Julian
    85, 110
Blackburne, Reverend Harry
    87
Bladen, Private F. Charles
    55, 67
Blair, Tony MP 134
Blundell, Private Richard
    69–70, 186–7
Bolton, Private Edward 54
Boos, Private F. 97
Bowerman, Private William
    97
Broadrick, Private Frederick
    110
Bray, Corporal Alan 51, 68,
    124–5
Browne, Des 139, 145, 179, 190

Burden, Private Herbert 130, 132, 149

Burrell, Private William 108–9

Byers, Private Joseph 42, 59–60, 139–41, 145, 148

Canadian Government 142–3

Carr, Private James 68

Carter, Private Henry 69

Cavinder, Sergeant Len 102

Chielens, Piet 60

Clarke, Mr H.V. 44

Collees, Dr John 59

Collins, Lieutenant 69,185

Concannon, Don MP 126

Cook, Robin MP 142–3

Conscientious Objectors 120–2

Crozier, Brigadier-General Frank 62, 64, 76–7, 84, 99, 113, 168

Crozier, Private James 62, 64, 77, 84, 167

Cunningham, Private Samuel 110

Dalande, Private Hector 90

Darling Committee 111, 168

Davids, Abraham 96

De Comyn, Andy 150

Dunn, Captain J.C. 124

Dyett, Sub-Lieutenant Edwin 21–2, 119

Earp, Private Arthur 40–1

Ellington, Lieutenant-Colonel 118

Esler, Captain M.S. 95

Evans, Private Andrew 59, 140

Farr, Private Harry 144, 150

Fellowes, Private Ernest 78

Field Punishment No. 1 30–2, 185

Field Punishment No. 2 32, 48, 160

Forbes, Lady Angela 104

Gameson, Captain L. 96–7

George V, King 118–19, 166, 169

Goggins, L/Cpl Peter 22, 49, 123

Graham, Private Stephen 51, 75

Guilford, Edward Montmorency 34, 38–9, 44, 46, 56, 64, 67, 77–8, 80, 82, 90, 93–5, 97, 100, 102, 160, 162

Haig, Sir Douglas 40–1, 75, 89, 103–4, 106, 114, 118, 142, 145, 151, 153, 164, 166–7, 186

Harris, Mrs Gracie 150

Harris, Private Willie 96

Hart, Private Benjamin 51–2

Hartells, Private Bert 78

Henderson, Douglas, MP 135

Highgate, Private Thomas 19, 27, 107–8, 118, 122, 148, 150

Hipkin, John 130–2, 138–9, 141, 193

Holmes, Private William 50–1, 65–6

Hoon, Geoff MP 142

Hunt, Private William 67, 75

Irish Government 23, 42, 119, 144

Ives, Corporal Frederick 78

Johnson, Private Frederick 161

Johnson Smith, Geoffrey MP 126

Jones, Mrs Anne Mary 80

Jones, Morgan 121

Kennedy, Private P.J. 56, 75

King's Regulations 11, 32, 34, 43, 50, 161

Kirk, Private Ernest 49

Kirman, Private Charles 124

Laister, John 70

Lamond, Lieutenant A.W. 54

Lewis, Corporal C. 91

Mackinlay, Andrew MP 130–1, 134–5, 137, 144, 147, 174, 190–3

Macready, Captain G. 78

Mainwaring, Lieutenant-Colonel 118

Major, John MP 131

Marshall, Albert 31

Mc Bride, Private Samuel 67

McClair, Private Harry 161

McColl, Private Charles 102

McCubbin, Private Bertie 123

McDonald, L/Cpl John 22, 48

Meyler, Lieutenant-Colonel H. 39, 125–6, 150, 163

Military Law, Manual of 30, 32, 34, 43

Morgan, Private Richard 87

Mohamed, Ahmed Mahmoud 105

Moore, Driver Thomas 19

Moran, Lord 60

Murphy, Private Patrick 53–4, 91–2

New Zealand Government 138, 142–3, 190

O'Neill, Private Frank 55, 95

Paterson, Second Lieutenant John 118

Phillips, Private H.T.W. 87–8

Price, L/Cpl William 87

Pridmore, Captain H.H. 77

Poole, Lieutenant Eric S. 116–18

Putkowski, Julian 127, 129–30, 136, 141, 161

Reeve, Private Harry 103–5

Reid, Private Isaac 51, 75–6

Reid, Dr John MP 135–7, 139, 146, 173, 188–9, 193

Richardson, Frank 60
Roberts, Private William 77
Robinson, Private John 78
Robinson, Lieutenant G.C., RAMC 67
Rochester, Private Albert 48–9
Rogers, Private John 78
Rogers, Captain T. Guy 87–8
Rose, Drummer Frederick 12

Sandbach, Charles 69, 182–3
Scholes, Private William 69
Scott, Canon F.G. 88–90, 102
Scotton, Private William 55
Silvester, Victor 70–1
Simpson, Keith MP 57, 112, 137, 144
Six, Marguerite 59
Skone, Private John 39
Slade, Private Frederick 76
Slack, Captain 52–3
Smith, Private James 182–5, 187–8, 193, 197
Smith-Dorrien, General Sir Horace 41–2, 108–9, 142, 148, 150
Southborough, Lord 112
Spellar, John MP 135
Steuart, Rev R.M.J. 90–1
Stormont-Gibbs, Captain 51–2

Tennant, Harold MP 111
Thompson, Alfred 78
Thurtle, Sir Ernest MP 45, 47, 49, 51, 53, 61, 68, 71, 112, 125–6, 147, 163
Tracey, Lieutenant G.D.C. 119
Troughton, Private Albert 87, 198
Turpic, Private William 55

Walkinton, Captain M.L. 53–4
Ward, Miss A.J., Head of Army Historical Branch 138
Ward, Private George 53, 72
Westmacott, Captain T.H. 54, 83
Williams, Private Henry 86
Williams, Private Walter 94, 109
Williamson, Father Benedict 91–2
Williamson, Rifleman Henry 68
Wood, Corporal Gordon 91
Wood, Major M.M. MP 114

Yeoman, Private Walter 85–6, 111

If you enjoyed this book, you may also be interested in…

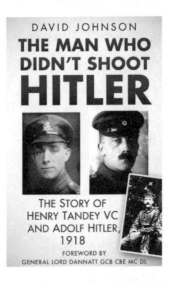

The Man Who Didn't Shoot Hitler

This is the tale of two men: Henry Tandey, an ordinary man later deemed to be 'a hero of the old berserk type' who emerged from the First World War as the most decorated British private to survive, and Adolf Hitler, who was highly decorated in his service to Germany in the First World War and went on to become one of the most infamous dictators in history.

The Man Who Didn't Shoot Hitler tells the story of Tandey's and Hitler's Great War, the moment when their lives became intertwined – if in fact they did – and how Tandey lived with the stigma of being known not for his chestful of medals, but as the man who let Hitler live.

978 0 7509 5362 7

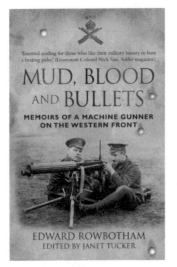

Mud, Blood and Bullets

It is 1915 and the Great War has been raging for a year when Edward Rowbotham, a coal miner from the Midlands, volunteers for Kitchener's Army. Drafted into the newly formed Machine Gun Corps, he is sent to fight in places whose names will forever be associated with mud and blood and sacrifice: Ypres, the Somme and Passchendaele. He is one of the 'lucky' ones, winning the Military Medal for bravery and surviving more than two and a half years of the terrible slaughter, which wiped out all but six of his original company. In these memoirs, the sights and sounds of battle, the excitement, the terror, the extraordinary comradeship, are all vividly described as if they had happened to him only yesterday.

978 0 7509 5661 1